ABOARD LCS 11
IN WW II

Aboard LCS 11 in WW II

A Memoir by Lawrence B. Smith

Edited by Kearney Smith, Ph.D.

Kearney Smith

To order additional copies of this book, contact:
Xlibris Corporation
1-888-795-4274
www.Xlibris.com
Orders@Xlibris.com
91705

CONTENTS

EDITOR'S PREFACE

There are really two stories about LCS 11 and her crew. This book contains the first story which is about a group of men from various backgrounds who came together largely by chance and by the whims of government planning. But they became a ship's crew, living and working together between 1944 and 1946. The other story, only hinted at in this book, is how they were reunited forty-odd years later and found that their initial impression that they liked each other was accurate, profound, and enduring. Their wives and extended families became a part of that second story which is revealed in a collection of more than two hundred and fifty shipmate newsletters and a string of reunions over a period of ten years.

The sources for this book are primarily the recollections and comments that appear in the newsletters that were printed and circulated beginning in June of 1987 by my brother Lawrence B. Smith. Other sources I have used are letters written by Lawrence to his brothers and sisters. The newsletters contain comments, remembrances, old letters, citations from diaries, and quotations from logs. The initiating topic of the newsletters is the experience of crewmen aboard a small warship during World War II. But a larger space is given to locating former shipmates and to discussing the lives of these veterans and their families years after the war.

In preparing this book, my goal was to establish a chronological narrative to frame the events described and alluded to by members of the crew of LCS 11. The narrative voice of my brother Lawrence was a natural choice since he initiated the reunion of the shipmates and published his and their remembrances in the newsletters. His way of writing the newsletter was to refer to subjects as they came to mind or as they were raised by his shipmates, rather than to explore one subject fully before moving on to another. As a result, instances of topics being raised and suspended occur throughout the newsletters. My work as editor was to collect these discussions from many places and put them together in a topical and chronological framework.

I had the pleasure of meeting some of the shipmates at one of their reunions. But by necessity, my information was limited since I was unable to interview members of the crew. In fact, I could not systematically discuss my brother's war experiences with him because his health was failing when I thought of taking up this project. But during the time of the shipmate reunions and the writing of the newsletters, Lawrence had known I was interested and had sent me copies of the newsletters as they were distributed.

Many of the sailors are good writers, and I am thankful for samples of their remembrances to include in this book. Also, I thank my wife, Catherine, for proof reading the manuscript.

Kearney Smith
Green Mountain, North Carolina
December 2010

Remembering the Day of Infamy

On Sunday, December 7, 1941, in Rowan County, North Carolina, six teenage boys followed their usual Sunday afternoon custom of hiking through the woods and fields of their parents' farms. I was one of these boys. We donned our old clothes after church, had Sunday dinner, and struck out for "the rocks and rills and wooded hills" beginning in front of the Mack and Mardre Smith farm and moving onto the farm of Uncle Will and Aunt Ruth Outen.

There were three Outen brothers and three Smith brothers in the group. The ages of myself and my brothers almost paralleled those of our cousins. I was 16 on April the 8th and Ernest Outen was 16 on July the 20th of that year. Jack Smith and Gene Outen were close to the same age, as were Paul Smith and Carl Outen. Just as we gathered behind Uncle Will's house, Carl and Paul decided they wanted to make bows and arrows. So they left the rest of us and went off toward the Little Bottom— one of the fields on my father's farm— to search along the Campbell Branch of Buffalo Creek for the bamboo canes they needed to make the shafts of their arrows.

Jack and I joined Ernest and Eugene and went to find out whether there was enough ice for skating in the creek bottom across from Morris' pasture. It had been very cold the night before, with temperatures well below freezing. So we were thinking of the narrow, long pond at the edge of the wooded hill to the south of the creek where two branches of Buffalo Creek joined. We were sure it would still be frozen over. The pond was in a low part of the bottom at the foot of the steep and high hill we called Deal's Hill. It was the same hill on which Daddy and his brothers and sisters did their sledding while living on the Jacob Deal Farm where the Joe Morris family moved in the 1930's. The pond was not deep, but it was ideal for ice skating. It was fed by wet-weather springs and stayed full of water most of the year, but especially in winter.

On our way to the pond we passed through the Old House Place on Uncle Will's land. It was the site of an old homestead that had belonged to Henry Goodman. Goodman had owned about one hundred and fifty acres of land which he sold to my father and his two brothers, Earl and Clyde, in the early 1920s. The three brothers had divided the land into three fifty-acre farms. Earl's farm was sold in the 1930's to my father's sister, Ruth, who had married Will Outen. The Goodman house had disappeared, but signs of the homestead were still visible to the discerning eye: the large walnut trees and the daffodils that grew around them each spring. And when plowing the surrounding land, the Outen boys often turned up shards of china in the black soil.

In those days, as boys will do, we prodded the dirt mounds in the fields and imagined that they were Indian burial sites. It was fun to speculate about the earlier explorers who had first built cabins in these woods and hunted deer and other large game no longer present in that part of North Carolina. That day we searched a thicket of wild boxwoods at the Old House Place because Ernest wanted to show us a large metal pulley wheel and spindle that he had discovered some time earlier. After we found and examined it, we decided it was part of some kind of sawmill or gristmill that had served the Goodmans or some earlier inhabitants of the old house.

It was also our custom to carve our initials on the slick, white bark of beechnut trees that grew along the creek bank. The largest of these beeches stood on rocky ground overlooking Uncle Will's water-driven ram pump that was powered by the water from the small creek. The pump ran constantly and pushed water from the old Goodman spring through a small buried pipe to the Outen house several hundred yards away.

Farther up Outen's creek, where the pasture opened out into a meadow, we usually built a pond each summer. Once it was full, our pond was about waist deep. The overflow of the creek ran through a ditch we dug in the hard bank to prevent the dam from breaking. Our ponds usually lasted through the summer or until a thunderstorm caused the creek to rise with more water than the overflow ditch could carry. Although the pond was really too small for swimming, it gave us a good place to cool off in summer and to wash the dust of the cotton fields out of our hair.

When we arrived in the bottom below Deal's Hill, we were pleased to find that the pond had indeed frozen. We ran onto it to begin skating, but the ice was not thick enough to hold us and cracked under our weight, and water got into our shoes. That didn't dampen our spirits. We yelled and laughed and cracked the ice by stamping our feet and running about on the shallow pond. When we grew tired and chilly, we went to high ground, pulled off our soaked shoes, and squeezed the water out of our socks.

Thin, high clouds streaked the sky, and the breeze was becoming cool. The daylight hours were drawing short when we arrived back at the Outen house. The Smith and Outen brothers parted near Uncle Will's honeybee boxes under the row of black gum trees that grew along the Outen's pasture fence near the barn. We were in sight of our house across the fields when Mama called to us from the front porch, "Lawrence, you boys come on home and do up the barn work." Then she added a puzzling remark. "The Japs have bombed Pearl Harbor."

Our usual Sunday night schedule left us some free time in the evenings after we had done our chores, which included milking the cows and putting hay in the stalls. If we convinced our parents we had no home work due at school the next day, they allowed us to listen to the Gene Autry radio show at 7 p.m. But that night, Jack and I were more interested in learning just what had happened at this place called Pearl Harbor.

When we turned on our little table-model Philco radio, we learned a few skimpy details of the bombing raids the Japanese had made on Pearl Harbor, Hawaii, and other places in the Pacific. We learned that the raid on Pearl Harbor had occurred about 12:30 p. m. our time. We then joined our cousins on the road midway between our homes There, we exchanged our thoughts on this news.

For a sixteen-year-old boy who thought any country was a fool to attack the United States, this turn of events was scary to contemplate. I took comfort in the fact that we were far enough inland from the ocean that war planes probably could not reach us. At that time we were unsure whether Germany was in on this sudden decision to start a war with us. Mom and Dad reassured us as we went to bed that night.

For Christmas that year, one of my presents was a diary book for 1942. It was about four by six inches in size, and the space that was provided for each date would allow me to write a short paragraph. I made entries every day that year and bought another book of the same size for 1943. I wrote in the second diary every day through late summer. But in the fall, I went into the Navy, and after that I didn't keep my diary as regularly.

A Country Boy in Boston

At the time of the Pearl Harbor attack, I was a sixteen-year-old student at Landis High School and a school bus driver. My cousins, my brothers, and I had formed the Lone Wolf Patrol as a chapter of the Open Road Pioneers, an organization similar to Boy Scouts, but without an adult leader. Also in our organization were Ray and Bill Beaver, two brothers who lived several miles away in Enochville. We had outings in my father's pasture where we cooked wieners over campfires, and built a hut of logs and slabs of bark which we had gleaned from local sawmill operations. In the diary that I was keeping at the time, I recorded our activities in school and on the farm. I was also the secretary for the Lone Wolf Patrol and kept minutes of our meetings. The first member of the Lone Wolf Patrol to go into military service in the spring of 1943 was Ray Beaver who joined the Army. When I turned eighteen, I went into the Navy. My cousin Ernest Outen, a few months younger than I, was drafted the same year. He decided that since Ray had gone into the Army and I had gone into the Navy, he would join the Marines.

I had boot camp training at the Bainbridge Naval Base in Maryland in the fall of 1943. Then I went home on boot leave for a week before returning to that station for training in radio. I made the following entries in my diary about that leave:

Monday, November 15, 1943

Today was cloudy and cold and a few pieces of sleet fell. We were paid at about 8:30 in the morning. We left Perryville about 9:30. I really had a train ride. I didn't enjoy it very much. A young fellow in the Army Air Corps made a good companion for me. We went down to the USO and got some free cookies, sandwiches, and coffee at Danville, Virginia. The train was sure crowded. I got up at 3 o'clock this morning to pack my sea bag. I got off the train at Salisbury and George brought me home. I woke up the whole family when I came in.

Tuesday, November 16, 1943

Today is clear and cold. I stayed around home today and talked with Mama and the young ones. Carol and Kenneth didn't know me very well, but by the end of today they did. I also slept a little and rested up because I spent 22 hours yesterday without much sleep.

Wednesday, November 17, 1943

Today is clear and pretty cold. I got in old 69 [the school bus I had driven as a student. My brother Jackie was now driving that bus.] and drove it all the way to school and parked it. I visited school nearly all day. I went to China Grove on the local bus and got a certificate to get 5 gallons of gas [gasoline was rationed]. I got off at Enoch and visited Grandma and also went up to the church where Daddy was working on the church tower. I went up on the church a little ways but decided not to go up to the top of the tower since I had my dress uniform on.

Thursday, November 18, 1943

Today is clear and really cold. Paul and Duane stayed out of school, and we went rabbit hunting. Although we didn't get anything, I enjoyed seeing the old scenery around home. It seemed very good just to see the places where I used to have such a good time hunting rabbits and crows and playing around. Aunt Ruth [Outen] gave a nice supper in my honor tonight. We had cake, ice cream, chicken and noodle soup.

Friday, November 19, 1943

I drove old 69 all the way to school today and caught the bus to Kannapolis. I had one large picture and 12 post card size pictures made. They cost me about $6.25. I met Albert Lawrence and we went to Landis School and we talked with the girls who work in the school store. They were the ones I worked with last year. Tonight Jackie and I went to Fred Freeze's house and we made some music. Harold Sechler was there.

Saturday, November 20, 1943

Today is clear and very warm. Uncle Pharr, Dad, and I went rabbit hunting. I ran up one out of the creek and Jackie missed it and quit hunting. We got six rabbits this morning. This evening we also got six. I sure did enjoy the hunt very much. I was glad to go over the old hunting ground again. I went to town this evening and saw the proofs of my pictures. They were very good. Violet Mae and Junie [daughters of Uncle Clyde, Daddy's brother] went along.

Sunday, November 21, 1943

Today is clear and warm. I went to our church again after missing a few Sundays. Mama and Aunt Cora Edith [Uncle Clyde's wife] had fixed a nice dinner. This evening Jackie and I went to Clyde Corriher's and Wayne Deal's house. I enjoyed visiting with these old pals. I went to choir practice with Daddy and Jackie this evening.

Monday, November 22, 1943

Today is warm and clear. I went to town with Daddy this morning. He got a new cross-cut saw. This evening I went to see George about the train schedule but he wasn't at home. I went to Kannapolis and found out about it and went to see the picture show "Rosie O'Grady." Mr. Swicegood, Hugh Brown, Paul Leonard Karriker, and Harry Starnes came to see me. Also Andrew Smith and Wilburn Overcash came by. I bought 5 gallons of gas allowed me today.

Tuesday, November 23, 1943

Today is clear and warm, but there is a pretty chilly north wind blowing. Well, the dreadful day has come at last, and back to Bainbridge I must go. I spent the morning with Dad and Mom and we went to Kannapolis and then I went with George to Salisbury about 2:30. We had a very tiresome trip [on the train] and I didn't enjoy any of it. I had to stand up between cars on the train.

Wednesday, November 24, 1943

I got to Washington at about 2:30 A.M. and Bainbridge at 6 A.M. It is very cold today. We washed some windows this morning. I learned that I really got Radio School. I slept on a cot tonight. But sailors going to a new assignment left this evening, and I will get a bunk in the morning. Our old company from boot camp is really scattered now.

When I returned to Bainbridge, I continued keeping a little diary although we were told in boot camp that we were not to have cameras or to keep diaries. I complied except for keeping one line notes of dates indicating when I started radio school or got leave or something else beyond the regular routine of events.

I was in the OGU (out going unit) where new recruits came in every day. They looked conspicuous in their bright colored civilian clothes, and I could shout: "You'll be sorry!" as others had yelled at me when I first came there as a raw recruit on September the 21st.

But I missed being home and tried to get there even on weekend liberty. So just nine days later on Friday, I was heading home on a train going to Washington and then to Greensboro. I was lucky in that respect. I didn't have to change trains at the Washington station. With so many servicemen traveling by train it was difficult to get aboard a train in the city. Even so I had to stand between the cars from Washington to Greensboro. I arrived in Kannapolis at 4:30 the next morning.

Daddy and Uncle Pharr went rabbit hunting that morning while my brother Jackie and I played harmonica and guitar. Later we walked over the vacant Henry Smith farmland that we had learned to love in our childhood. That night I visited the home of my father's cousins Claude and Florence Smith who lived on an adjoining farm.

The next day I went to St. Enoch Lutheran Church in Enochville with my family. Right after church, my Dad gave me a ride to Kannapolis where I had to catch a train back to Maryland. I didn't know the train schedule and had to wait until 4:30 p. m. I didn't reach the front gate at Bainbridge until 6:40 in the morning. I was detained at the gate and was told that I knew better than to go more than a hundred miles on a weekend pass. They assured me that I had been told this earlier, but I didn't remember it.

I was planning another trip home for Christmas. On Friday, December the 24th I had a 72-hour pass liberty and caught a special train to Washington at 1:15 p. m. I was going to have to wait until 5:30 to catch another train to Kannapolis. So having a couple of hours to kill, I walked downtown, which turned out to be a big mistake. When I returned to Union Station about 5 o'clock, there were about 5 thousand servicemen in that huge building. I had bought my ticket earlier and I tried to move to the stairway that led down to the track level.

Servicemen were now massed all around me, and when I took my wallet out of my peacoat to get my ticket, a bunch of change fell out of it. But people were packed so tightly around me that I could not bend over to retrieve this money. Finally, I got down the stairs to the train and saw sailors pulling other sailors onto the train through the open dining car windows. Since I didn't know any of these people at the windows of the train, I waited to get on through the doors. Then suddenly MPs and SPs came and blocked the doors and windows, announcing that no more people could board the train.

That such a thing could happen had not crossed my mind. It was Christmas Eve, and I had never spent Christmas away from home. Through ignorance, I thought they would get a second train or something. No, I was told, there were no more trains. I went to the Station window and got a refund on my ticket to Kannapolis. Needless to say, I was feeling pretty low and was wondering what I should do next.

Lo and behold, I looked up and saw James Thurman Turnipseed, Jr., from Columbus, Mississippi, and John Sawyer from Washington, North Carolina. Both had been in the same company with me in boot camp. They had missed the train too and were wondering what they were going to do. We walked up and down and around and tried to console each other about missing our first Christmas at home.

Finally we got something to eat and began looking for a place to sleep. Up until that time we had not been on liberties in cities and did not know about the USO and churches which arranged for cots in basements, and so forth, as sleeping places for servicemen. So we went in an old hotel, a little narrow building with the desk at the front door. It was run down and didn't have many rooms. Our room had a couple of beds and a big steam radiator under a window which was covered by a tan shade.

I remember lying awake for hours. The next morning we missed seeing our little brothers and sisters pulling toys from under a Christmas tree. I lay there looking at the cracked ceiling, listening to that awful screeching and grinding of those electric street cars as they ground along the empty streets on this cold, dreary morning. I reached over and pulled back the old shade and saw that it had snowed, sleeted, and frozen over during the night.

We spent most of the day at a USO and my diary says, "I went to some picture shows. I am sure it is my most unhappy Christmas. If I had tried harder to get home, I would have felt better." I spent the following night at the USO and got some nice presents. The next day, Sunday, the 26th I caught the train back to camp at 4:30 p. m. My diary says that I sent a box of candy home to my folks—Hersheys I had bought at Perryville.

I was becoming accustomed to riding the train because I would now get liberties some weekends and catch the train to Baltimore or Washington. I also formed a friendship with George Jones of Lancaster, Pennsylvania, and the two of us would go to his home some weekends. Somehow we later started getting liberty on different weekends, but I would go by myself to spend weekends with his parents .

Because I had not been home for Christmas, my Mom decided that my brother Jackie should come to Washington to visit me. And he came for a weekend. I can't remember where we slept Friday and Saturday nights, but I do remember we went to one of those penny arcades that one sees on streets near train stations and in recreational parts of town. It was something like the game arcades of later times with video games. We looked around at the various entertainment devices. One of the gimmicks was a box with a handle for each hand. The object was to squeeze the handles to make a needle in a gauge register a high number. At the same time an electric shock entering the hands increased as the handles were squeezed harder.

I tried it first and set a high mark. Then Jackie took over and squeezed those handles so hard that the electric shock wouldn't let him turn loose. The pain was very severe, and he jerked the contraption off the wall and flung it to the floor. As it crashed down, batteries and other pieces scattered over the floor. The proprietor came running over. He was furious and threw us out of the place, but not before calling us country hicks and worse names. I guess he knew we didn't have enough money to pay for the machine. He didn't press charges or have us taken to jail.

On March the 23rd, while I was in radio school, I and some other sailors were called to a meeting and told that our grades on tests we had taken some time earlier qualified us for officer training school. I was interested, but the next day I received a telegram from the Red Cross that said my Dad had pneumonia and I was permitted to take an emergency leave. I went home for five days. My Dad got well, Thank God, and I returned to base. While I was gone, the draft for officer training had been called up and had gone, so I missed my chance of becoming an Admiral.

On May the 22nd, I graduated from radio school at Bainbridge. On the 26th I was sent with a group of other men to Little Creek, Virginia. I can't remember whether it was a bus or a train that we boarded for our new duty station, but we came to Cape Charles, Virginia, at the southern tip of the long strip of territory that lies across the Chesapeake Bay from the rest of Virginia. We boarded one of those impressive ferries that plied that route prior to the building of the bay-bridge-tunnel. The vessel seemed huge, and this was like the first Navy trip to sea for some of us farm boys. We climbed to the highest point forward and lolled around on our sea bags as we felt that, at last, we were really in the Navy. Man, we almost got out of sight of land on this twenty-or—so mile trip! It was a beautiful spring day and it was as if we were on a lark.

Upon arrival I was sent to the little Creek Amphibious Base. I went on my first liberty in Norfolk on June the 4th, and several of us went to the Gaiety Theater where we saw girls doing some risque dancing. We also went up to the Ocean View Amusement Park beside the Chesapeake Bay and took some of the rides.

Again on the night of June the 5th a bunch of us country boys were up town. We were told that a "Grand Ole Opry" show for servicemen was being performed in a big auditorium. We couldn't get in the 8 p.m. performance and milled around until the 10 p.m. show. We enjoyed that and when we came out at midnight, we heard an awful noise of sirens and whistles. We thought the Germans had landed at Norfolk. So we went into a police station and learned that the American forces had landed on the coast of France.

In the wee hours of the morning we took a trolley to Ocean View Park and walked the five or six remaining miles to the Little Creek base. We arrived just in time for breakfast and then stood at parade rest all day while yeomen and assorted officers walked up and down and called out our names to form up crews. It was the first time I had ever slept standing up. While slumping in my tracks at parade rest, the crew lists were called out. That's when I learned I was on the LCS 11 roster.

On June the 8th, I was assigned to the crew of USS LCS (L) amphibious support ship which was being constructed at Boston. At the Amphibious Base the communications gang for our ship was put together. The radar men, quartermasters, signalmen, and radiomen came a crew unit there. Sid Darion, Willis Rogers, Bill Fandel, G. O. Davis, and others who ultimately served on LCS 11, started training together at the time.

Few of the crew members had any real idea what this LCS 11 would be like. We learned later it was especially designed and built as a shallow-draft gun ship to support Marines landing on hostile shores. It was heavily armed to give continuous fire support to landing craft and to fire on land targets after the Marines were ashore.

We did know that the LCS was designed on the same basic keel as an LCI which most of us had seen in newsreels or first-hand. On July the 28th our crew went aboard LCI 576 for a week's training in the Chesapeake Bay. It was a prelude to being on our own ship. But I am amazed that I remember so little about the LCI and what we did aboard her. I suppose during the week we learned that our new ship was going to be something like it.

Since the war, the National Association of LCS's has published a note in which Captain Frank Adams explains how the LCI is related to the LCS: "Approximately one year before the LCS (L)s were built, the Navy sent 12 LCI's to New Meia, New Caledonia, to be converted into gun boats. They put 40mm and 3" guns on the 12, and we were then primarily attached to PT squadrons. I understand that it was the success of these LCI's that prompted the construction of the LCS (L)'s. My ship was the "69," and I do not remember the other numbers, but a good many of the skippers of the old LCI's, on return to the States, were attached to the LCS group as I was." Sit Darion thinks we may have had a three inch gun on LCS 11 in the early days, but by the time we entered battle the rocket rack had replaced the big gun.

On August the 4th after a week of training on the Chesapeake Bay, we went ashore at Solomons Naval Base and took a bus to Washington, D. C. At about 11 p. m. that same night our crew boarded a train for Boston where we would eventually take charge of our new ship. While waiting for our train in the Washington railway station, some of our crew went to the bathroom and pushed a couple of smaller guys through the windows on a mission to get some booze. This beverage was to add a lot of spirit to our trip. Being a teetotaler, I tried to get some sleep in my berth. It was no use. As the party got more lively, shouts and loud versions of "Anchors Aweigh"(and more bawdy songs) rang out, and I was repeatedly offered a swig from the bottles. Finally a couple of Shore Patrolmen came through and helped settle things down, but there wasn't much night left for sleeping. We arrived that morning, August the 5th, in Boston, and we were billeted in the Fargo Building at 495 Summer Street.

Shipmate Frank Krishko remembers "our trip via troop train to the Fargo Building in Boston, as I was selected for baggage detail upon arrival, which turned out to be a big plus." Frank continues:

Since we arrived on a Saturday morning, those who were on baggage detail were given a weekend liberty. The glitch was I was broke, having less than two bucks in my pocket. I sorta hung around since I was short in the cash department. Walking into the head that Saturday afternoon, I found a crap game going on. After watching the game a while, I started to make little side bets, a quarter here and a quarter there. After a bit I accumulated a little stake and was offered the dice. Consequently, I built my two bucks into ninety dollars. I can say that is the only time in my Naval career I won any money.

Also staying in the Fargo Building were a great many other American as well as British sailors. As soon as I had been assigned a bunk, I went on a liberty that lasted till 0800 on Monday the 7th. During the six weeks I was stationed in Boston, I became familiar with certain parts of the city. George Robert Waldron, a native of Brockton, was not yet a member of our crew, so I didn't have the benefit of his knowledge as a tour guide. I remember Scully Square, and on my own I found the Boston Commons. It was a nice park like some of the ones I knew back in North Carolina, with a bandstand on the high ground, and a little lake with ducks.

While shopping in a business section of the city, I found an electronics store where I looked at a gadget for practicing code, and I examined other radio items. My letters to my brother Jackie had been, so far, largely about my schooling in radio and code. He had become interested in radio too, and back home he was building transmitters and receivers and learning code. When I was on leave a few times, I found he had rigged up some little boxes with wires running from our farm-house dining room up to the sleeping quarters on the second floor. Using flashlight batteries we were able to send each other messages in Morse code. So I looked for items I could recommend to him.

One night a young shoeshine boy hounded me to get a shoeshine. He put forth a hard sell. Finally he said, "If I can't tell you in which state you were born, the shoe shine is free." I took a seat and put my feet on the shoe rest. Well, I thought the guy had discerned a North Carolina accent and decided to test him. The little guy kept up a running prattle. I thought that was to get me to talk, so I said as little as possible, hoping to save myself ten cents. When the shine was ended, he very smugly said, "You were born in the state of infancy!"

While stationed at Boston, I met Ernie Moore, called "Jo-Jo," by his friends. Ernie was from New York State. He was a radio technician on LCS 12 and with our common interest in radio, we became friends. In those days the song, "I Met a Million-Dollar Baby in a Ten-Cent Store," was popular, and one day Jo-Jo told me he had met a couple of such girls in a ten-cent store—Woolworth's— and he wanted to introduce me to one of them. That was how I met Margaret Carlson on August 10th. We dated for about a month before I shipped out. Margaret lived in the Roslindale neighborhood at 27 Cotton Street (which I figured was a good omen because I had picked right much cotton). She introduced me to some of her favorite places. One of these was some pretty woods she called the Arboretum.

Margaret told me this arboretum was connected with Harvard University in some way. Occasionally we walked there from her house, which wasn't far. She and I spent quite a bit of time together. I took liberty sometimes every night. We saw lots of movies and spent time touring the Boston suburb, Roslindale.

Shake-Down Cruise

My diary entry for September the 10th says that we moved from Fargo Building to Neponset Point where the George Lawley & Sons Shipyards were located and where our ship LCS 11 was being completed. I lived on subsistence, meaning that I was on my own in providing meals and housing. There I lived in a nice little room on the upper floor of a plank home. In the radio section Charles Hammond, Robert Faller, and I had the job of protecting the radio equipment aboard the new ship. We familiarized ourselves with the radio shack, a place we would spend thousands of hours in the coming months. We wore 45 pistols at our waist as took turns standing watch. One day when Hammond was on duty, a civilian barged into the radio shack, and Chuck jammed his automatic into the guy's belly. The poor fellow begged for mercy until a top official came on the scene and assured Hammond that the man was not a threat to our equipment.

The full designation of our little ship was USS LCS "Landing Craft Support (Large) No. 11." She was commissioned and launched on Wednesday, September the 13th. We began living aboard at that time. Between September the 13th and 25th the guys went on liberty almost every night. I rode streetcars or buses from Neponset Point to downtown Boston or Dorchester. But Margie didn't seem to have time for dates during that period of time. The reason for it, I learned, was that her mother didn't allow her to go out with guys who were nearing the time to be shipped out.

Some time after LCS No 11 had been commissioned, a hurricane came up the coast and made that little ship tug at her lines. Our deck hands had the job of checking, loosening, and tightening different lines all night long as the storm passed through. They did a good job and no damage was done. But this learning experience was not much help to us a year later when we had the scare of our lives in a typhoon off the coast of Okinawa.

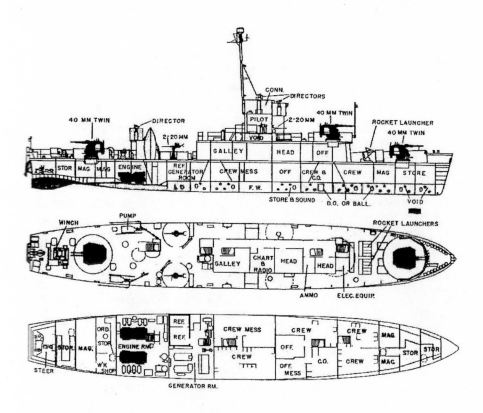

Schematic of LCS 11

During these days before leaving Boston, I was getting used to the layout of LCS 11. Only cooks were allowed in the galley, a small narrow room at the top of the ladder leading down to our mess hall. Food was ladled onto our trays as we walked past the galley door. If we asked for more potatoes or pretended to be unhappy at the sight of certain foods, the guys on mess duty would threaten to withhold food from our trays.

As a country boy, I was accustomed to grits, potatoes, green beans, cornbread, and other plain dishes. I didn't expect fancy food and had no complaints about the food served on our ship. One dish in particular I remember liking was the stew made by John T. Lynn, our chief cook. I recall only a couple of times aboard LCS 11 when there were any problems getting chow. We once had to eat canned or dried food for a couple of days when our steam cooking apparatus failed. We were on our way back from Shanghai and the steam generator wouldn't operate. That was the time when Corpsman Curtis Dobbs, our "Doc" from Opelika, Alabama, let the radio shack gang use his electric sterlizer to boil eggs and to cook other food.

By and large, our food aboard ship was very good. But during the battle of Okinawa the next spring, our duties sometimes interfered with our meals. I remember several times getting up too late for breakfast and having to improvise. On those days we would enjoy eating toast near the coffee urns. That was when we had delicious jelly and jam dipped from gallon cans that had been shipped from Australia.

About those times, G. O. Davis says, "I was the mail man and put Lynn's mail in his locker. In return Lynn put cinnamon buns in my locker. When we were in the Pescadores Islands, cutting and plowing up the mines, we had to go ashore because a storm came up. We went to a hospital and a Chinese doctor showed us around. In the lab they had unborn babies in jars and our cook, whose name I can't remember, was looking at the jars. The doctor came over and took the lid off so he could get a better look, and the cook took off like a shot. I remember the way he looked. He had a ruddy, round face and was short and stocky, and he worked under John Lynn, our chief cook."

I think our daily shipboard routines were regulated a little more sternly than on other ships. But despite some occasional gripes, our crew's *esprit de corps* was better because of the discipline aboard our ship.

On September the 25th, LCS 11 under the command of M. E. White sailed from Boston. We steered for our next duty station back at Norfolk, Virginia. That part of our cruise was a "black-out trip," meaning that the ship was running without lights. My notes show that we were hearing popular songs of the day on our radio— songs such as "Long Ago and Far Away," "A Lovely Way To Spend An Evening," "Amour," and "Straighten Up and Fly Right."

Only a quartermaster could love all the bearings, course changes, speed changes, and distances to buoys listed in our deck log for September the 25th, 26th, and 27th. But I enjoyed the trip through the Cape Cod Canal. It gave a landlubber like me a link with land. Our log for the 27th shows we entered the Little Creek channel at 0937 hours. After an inspection party boarded the ship and checked us out, we got underway again at 1129. The log says we had a communication exchange with USS BB-17. By 1920 hours we were moored alongside an LCI at the south side of Pier 9 at Solomons Naval Base.

Captain White and the Radio

The next day we began preparing our new little ship, the Eleven, for sea by going through maneuvers in the Atlantic off Little Creek, Virginia. At 0700 we fueled the ship, taking on 15,237 gallons of diesel fuel. According to our deck log, our forward draft changed by 1 foot and 1 inch, and the stern changed 1 inch. We were then inspected by the Officer in Charge. On Friday, September the 27th, we performed other maneuvers such as firing our guns and laying smoke-screens. I must have slept through the "expending" of 400 rounds of 40mm, 488 rounds of 20mm, and 5 pyrotechnics that the ship log records.

Next, we had various formation exercises in the company of other ships. Keeping station with the other ships turned out to be unpleasant for members of our ship's crew—-and I guess, especially for our skipper. For this part of our shakedown cruise, I was in the wheel house on a remote radio mike, passing along different commands, such as "mark," and "execute," to our skipper from the group commander in another ship. Evidently our quartermasters had used the wrong code books, a mistake that caused our ship to be zigging when it should have been zagging. The commander in charge of maneuvers on the command ship soon forgot about "overs" and "outs," and other radio protocols.

When our ship continued to make the wrong moves, the group commander said to me by radio phone, "Radioman, tell your skipper to turn the right way on the command to execute." Well, I wasn't about to start telling my skipper what to do and certainly not in the tone of voice the commander used. I became very distressed for Mr. White because I knew our failure to maneuver correctly wasn't his fault. But if I had done what the commander told me to do, it would have sounded as though I was running the ship and the captain was manning the wheel. I was not about to do that. Finally, the commander said, "Sailor, put your captain on the radio." When I advised him that the commander wanted him on the radio, Mr. White came down from the conn to take the microphone.

But that was not the end of our problem. We had switched the radio to a speaker that allowed everyone in the wheel house to hear. Moreover, our radio setup posed a problem for Mr. White. At that time we had the TCS AM radio which could receive signals from a great distance but with low output wattage would not transmit as far. It could be used for either code or voice transmissions as needed. But, more importantly, it used the same antenna for both sending and receiving. This meant that the operator would press the mike button to transmit a message but had to release it to receive a message. That is not a difficult concept in recent years with the widespread use of CB and HAM radio, but at that time most people had no experience with that arrangement.

When the commander had finished his insulting remarks to our captain, he waited for a reply. I showed Mr. White that he needed to press the mike button to speak and release it to listen. Our skipper made his statement, but under stress he continued gripping the mike with white knuckles, preventing our radio from receiving the reply from the commander. When I reached and tried to pull Mr. White's fingers off the transmit button, he gave me a look as if to say, "Keep your hands off mine unless you want to walk the plank." I understood the stress he was feeling and gently repeated, "Captain, to receive you need to release the transmit key."

There was lots of noise and confusion. I was probably more anxious about this confusion than he was. But our skipper had far more to answer for than did these young sailors if the worst happened and we had a collision. After Mr. White's conversation with the group commander, we started using the right code and began to zig and zag correctly. But I hated that our skipper looked bad because of the errors of our young, inexperienced crew. I thought, too, that the commander could have been more understanding about this screw up.

Later in our cruise aboard the Eleven, we had our complaints against Mr. White. Many of us were just teenagers not more than 18 or 19. We griped about our skipper in the same way we griped about the food. But to maintain discipline and authority, a commander must remain somewhat aloof, having less friendly ways than he himself might prefer. I have heard praise for our skipper from the officers and the enlisted men in our crew. Many of us know that Captain White's judgement and seamanship pulled us through that night of terror in the typhoon. As Blair Vedder puts it, "He was one helluva skipper. You always knew where you stood with him."

LCS 11 GOES TO SEA

We returned to port for a few days after our sea trials for some adjustments. On October the 11th Navy Yard repairmen came aboard. A diver removed thirty feet of 3/4 inch line from the starboard screw. Also there were replacements in the crew up to the time we sailed. A new crewman, Russell Warren Mace, came aboard the day before we sailed out of Norfolk on the 21st. Our ship was in formation with four other LCS's and a converted LCI. The converted LCI was the commanding ship and an officer aboard her was in charge of the group. Lt. M. E. White, Captain of LCS 11, was in charge of three LCS's: 11, 12, and 13. We were on a heading south down the Atlantic Coast bound for Key West, Panama, and the Pacific coast.

Our ship had a small group of radiomen. When it was first commissioned, Chuck Hammond, Robert A. Faller and I made up the radio staff. And that wise-cracking, twinkle-eyed Sid Darion was our best (only) radio technician. He kept the radio and radar in operating condition. At Hawaii, Bernard L. Michaelson became a part of our communications crew. But later when Mr. White was given command over the group of LCS's, Michaelson moved with him to the command ship. Mike stood watches in rotation with our regular radio crew while he was aboard our ship.

The Radio Shack was only about 9 feet by 9 feet, with one corner taken away by the ladder well up to the wheel house. This little room also had a desk with a stool for the quartermaster when he wanted to work with his charts. There were desk drawers, but charts were piled on the desk up to the ceiling. The radioman on duty also had a chair and a desk at the radio equipment mounted on the bulkhead above it. The radar man, Curtis "Tex" Pace, had a chair in his little corner so he could peer at the SO-2 screen.

A depth finder was wedged in there, too. In the beginning we had some unused space behind the radar man in the other corner, but something was installed there later. I guess it was a basketball court! A voice tube ran up the wall by the radar man's chair so he could shout up to the conning tower and give distances to the Jap suicide boats, rocks, or shore. He could also report the depth of the water as we neared a reef. Even with all this gear, there were times when we had nine or ten men in the shack for bull sessions.

Chuck, Bob, and I stood watch four hours on and eight hours off around the clock. During general quarters all of us had duties regardless of whether it was our time to stand radio watch. As we sailed down the East Coast that fall, a radioman on duty was required to copy code during all four hours of his watch whether the message was directed to our ship or not. All this time listening to radio traffic gave us a lot of practice copying code. Since a ship the size of an LCS had only three or four radiomen and a minimal amount radio equipment, we were allowed to close down our radio watch duties while anchored or tied up to a pier at a Naval base.

Messages sent by signal lights were more secure than radio transmissions, and ships in close proximity to each other used lights. Only ships in peril would transmit on radio at sea because German subs were "all ears" for a signal from a ship that they could zero in on, stalk, and torpedo. In radio school we had been told that the Germans and Japs had men who listened so intently to Morse code from American ships that they were able to identify the source of the messages. They were able to do that because they recognized the way certain operators "rattled" or "jazzed up" or otherwise personalized their sending of code. As I recall, we radiomen on LCS 11 rarely had the opportunity to send a serious message via CW or Morse code. After we got FM radios installed at Hawaii, most messages between ships were passed by voice because these transmissions traveled only line-of-sight distances.

Big radio facilities on the Atlantic coast sent messages about weather and other matters to ships almost constantly. Radiomen aboard all the ships in our formation were copying the Ship-to-Shore frequency of 2716 kilocycles in CW. "Shore-to-ship" would have been a better name for it because we were not transmitting, but all ships sailing the Atlantic were copying from NSS (Washington); NAS (Norfolk); Charleston; Jacksonville; or Key West Naval Stations. The frequency was flooded with messages. Many signals could be heard on adjacent frequencies with only a slight turn of the radio dial. Turning the dial less than a quarter of an inch yielded a dozen or so transmissions.

Prolonged copying of the 2716 frequency was rather boring for us because all the messages came through in sets of 5 letters or numbers which were meaningless to us. The messages had to be decoded by our communications officer before they could be understood. From time to time we would receive messages of general interest to most of our ships about weather and other routine matters. Code words stood for such things as water, ammunition, diesel fuel, and amounts of these things. So our report sounded something like this: "pumpkins x-ray, jig, king, oboe; muscadines: able charlie dog how."

It was up to the radioman to tune his radio to copy NSS, and other stations where these messages originated. Late at night NSS would have no real traffic to send but sent a repeated signal which was apparently a recording. It would sing out, "Dah-dit, ditty-dit, ditty-dit" over and over so that any radioman on duty would know he was on the right frequency and that no real traffic was being sent at present. These main transmitting stations like NSS would jingle their key to wake up any tired radioman on duty who needed to be alerted for a message.

Generally the messages I copied began with the heading dah-dit, dit, dit-dah-dit, dah-dit-dah (NERK) dit-dit-dit-dah (V meaning "from") and then dah-dit, ditty-dit, ditty-dit (NSS). These were part of the heading indicating what kind of information was in the message. The complete heading coming before the body of the message looked something like this: NERK V NSS OP-F-45 BT: The body of the message following the heading would be something like this: SZRTX MYLPW WNHTY JYTRS JKRPT LYRCK MNOHY SZYTR MRTYE BT.

NERK stood for "all ships and stations"; V meant "from"; NSS stood for the station sending the message. OP meant "operational priority" and indicated an important message about operations and dangers. An O in the heading meant "Urgent," or "extremely important." P meant "priority" and was ranked below O and OP but above R which meant "routine." A routine message would be general information about things like supplies. An F in the heading meant "Do not answer" or that no reply was needed or expected, and we called it a "Fox" message. Usually messages to little ships like ours were Fox messages. We didn't transmit unless there was some emergency that required the breaking of radio silence.

There was one exception. Every evening about dark each ship used the TCS AM Radio to send a logistic report to the commanding ship. The radio could receive long-distance messages, but this report was sent in voice mode at low power that produced a limited transmission range of about 20-25 miles.

Cape Hatteras Message

October 22, 1944, turned out to be "Sea Sick Sunday" on our ship. We had just passed the Cape Hatteras Light at 0624. At that location the Outer Banks jut out into the ocean, and the cold northern currents clash with the warm southern ones, causing rough and stormy seas. Because of the numerous ship wrecks that have occurred there, the ocean off the coast of North Carolina is sometimes referred to as the Graveyard of the Atlantic. We didn't get a storm there, but the water was really rough. It had its effect on many of our crew who were like young children just let off a merry-go-round that had spun out of control for half an hour.

All day our fellows had been plagued with seasickness. Some were hanging their heads over the side, waiting for the next wave of nausea to have its effect. Others lay moaning about the deck. Doc Dobbs was like a mother hen tending her flock as he passed out dry soda crackers and advice. He told those not on duty to stay on deck, reminding them that fresh air would be better for them than the stale air and fumes down below.

I had the 2000 to 2400 watch in the radio shack the next day. All the ships in our group were "guarding" or copying the Ship-to-Shore frequency. We were alert for any message that included our call letters. As leading radioman, I had to see that all call signs for appropriate ships were encoded and listed on our ready sheet for reference. So I encoded our ship's call sign and that of LCS 12, LCI 713, LCI 813, LCI 814, as well as the division commander's own command sign. We didn't break radio silence except for giving our logistic report to the commander's radioman at 1930 each night. That was on voice radio. The code name for LCS 11 at that time was "Talmud 1." We would say, "This is Talmud 1, stand by for logistic report." And then we used code words for water, fuel, and so forth, and gave the number of gallons in code letters. That night I continued working in the radio shack, proud that I had been tough and had not really been seasick. Then as I was preparing to give the voice logistic report, a wave of nausea hit me. I had just made radio contact with the commanding ship and said, "Standby for logistic report," when I had to reach for the wastebasket. But I did recover enough to continue the report.

Probably around 10:30 p.m. as I was copying the Ship-to-Shore frequency, I suddenly became aware that I was copying a message directed to our division commander, and it was an urgent message. It read something like this: MRVQV NAS-O-F-BT AVCHR MKLTZ ZYMPT RVKLX GRDEL MVCWK ZAQWE RTYUI QPASD FGHJK LZXCV BNMQA BT 10221030 G. Then I heard "dit dit, dah dah, dit dit." This spells IMI which means the message is being repeated. So I copied the entire message again and saw that it was coming from the Norfolk Naval Base.

In just a minute or two after the end of the second copying of the message, here it came again and this time it was coming from the Naval Station at Charleston, S. C. I copied it twice and tried to get it perfectly each time. I was getting excited. I copied it a third and a fourth time. A few minutes later here comes the message again, this time from Naval Air Station at Jacksonville, Fla. So I copied the message two more times. I was so thrilled that I wrote on the edge of the log sheet: "GUARANTEED PERFECT" in red ink.

Since the message was addressed to the commander of our group in his personal call sign, I did not think it was appropriate to break radio silence to call him or his radioman, or ask the LCS signalman to send a blinker light to his ship which was steaming along at the point of our wedge-shaped formation. I believed that the commander was at this time consulting with his communications officer and decoding the message, but it was a big thrill for me to copy an urgent message. Most of the messages I had copied were routine if they involved our ship. Robert A. Faller relieved me at midnight and I went to my sack feeling pretty good about getting that message and having copied it exactly.

The next day Ensign Frederick J. Henry, Jr., our communications officer, came into the radio shack and looked around and picked up our radio log and flipped back through the pages. On seeing my red penciled notation, "Guaranteed Perfect," he said, "What's this?" With some pride I explained that this was an urgent message to our commander that I had copied six times last night and in six tries I was sure I got it perfect. He nodded and said no more.

Two nights later, in the wee hours of October the 25th, we passed close to Miami Beach. The lights on shore were very bright for several miles. We were traveling without lights and it seemed strange. As I check our deck log, I conclude we were passing there around 0203 on October the 25th since the log entry says we "took a bearing on Fowery Rocks light, distance two and one half miles to starboard." I suppose that any German subs were seaward of us, were squinting through their periscopes and remarking at the parade of powerful warships—LCS's!

Urgent Message Deciphered

At mid-morning October the 26th we turned due west heading into Key West and about noon we altered course slightly to the south, bringing a brisk wind into our faces. I stood in front of the wheel house or conning tower as we neared the port. I was amazed at the steady pressure of the wind in my face. It almost blew my eyelids shut. At 1500 we moored alongside LCI 810. Before we were allowed to go on liberty, we got Federal ballots for the upcoming election. Then the starboard section, to which I belonged, was allowed to go on liberty. Paul Weir and Tom Taylor of Purvis, Mississippi, went ashore together.

Paul recalls that "When we were in Key West, Tom Cat and I went on liberty. We got a few drinks in us and purchased a case of beer to take on board for later. The Marines or SP would not let us on the base with it. They said we would have to leave it. Tom said he would drink it and take it in that way. So we walked down along the fence a ways, sat down and proceeded to try to polish off that case. I don't remember how we got aboard ship or how much we left in the case."

I went on liberty too and found that a small carnival was playing. Some sailors were pitching pennies and buying hot dogs. I joined them and noticed across the way some radiomen from LCS 12 and from other ships. I shouted over to them and asked, "Did you receive that urgent message a couple of nights ago?" They looked perplexed and said, "No."

Their communications officer was in the group and became interested. He came over to me and asked for details about the message. After I described it to him, he suggested that we go to my ship and get a copy and check it out. This officer was something of a "regular Joe," and after we got permission from our officers to take a copy to his ship, he permitted me to go along and to watch as he decoded the message. The decoding was interesting to me. It required a special board on which strips were moved about to show what each letter stood for.

The message came out something like this: "Proceed to Lat. 37 deg. 6 minutes and Long. 75 deg. 1 min. Search for survivors from torpedoed ship." After 43 years I am not sure of these reference points and do not know if the name of the torpedoed ship was mentioned in the message. But the message sent a chill down my spine. Apparently our group of ships had been in the best position to search for survivors, but the message never reached the commanding officer. I do not know if this communication officer went to the commander with it. But to me it was sad, and I hoped none of our fellow naval personnel had lost their lives because of this "missed" message.

Missed signals sometimes played a fairly important part in battles of the war and on occasion gave our side an advantage. In the Midway battle a Japanese destroyer turned wrong and damaged a major Japanese ship. In the case of the Cape Hatteras missed message, I like to think some other US ships and planes spotted the survivors the next day and rescued them. We should not severely fault the radiomen on that LCI command ship because the 2716 frequency was extremely crowded with signals. Still, it was the duty of radiomen to copy the signals from the major shore stations like NSS. For my part, I promised myself I would raise a ruckus in the future to make sure such a message that I might copy would be delivered into the appropriate hands.

I think it interesting that after all of the hours of practice in copying Morse code messages, we used voice radio exclusively in close convoys and in the battle of Okinawa. Undoubtedly the messages were mainly of short-term significance and would be of little value to the enemy. We did have fun trying to copy plain language messages in Morse code. Chuck had a sort of wicked way with the sending key when we practiced sending messages at Boston and at the Chesapeake Bay. The jazzy operators were referred to as "key jockeys."

On Friday, October the 27th, at 0830 we cast off lines and got underway for the Panama Canal Zone. The ship's log says Adam E. Carter was awarded Deck Court, charged with AOL for 73 hours and 35 minutes. I believe we were given sheathed knives prior to our arrival at Key West, and they were taken away from us prior to our arrival at Cristobal, Canal Zone. Perhaps after the Key West liberties, it was decided to retrieve them until we faced some Japs.

I remember we had a slightly rough sea en route to the Canal, and I saw my first flying fish. Every day many of them seemed to want to serve on the Eleven, but they were swept off the deck each morning. About noon on October the 31st we moored alongside LCS 12 at Coca Solo Base. The log does not record and I do not remember any tricks we played that Halloween night.

After going ashore on liberty on Thursday, November the 2nd, I passed a fresh fruit stand where I saw bananas that appeared to be about 18 inches long. They looked good. I had never had all the bananas I could eat at one time. So I bought 10 cents worth which amounted to about eight bananas. I ate all I could and left the remainder in a brown bag on a dime store counter. Kellogg and I walked around Colon and had our pictures taken at a photograph establishment.

Then we came upon Cash Street and circled the block. Around this block families lived in stucco apartments. At the steps in the little yards sat the Mama and Papa, and their daughter stood at the edge of the yard, asking sailors to come inside. I decided that Cash was an appropriate name for this street. These were new experiences for me. I had never before seen parents openly sending their daughters out to solicit men.

According to our log, on November the 3rd a merchant vessel, while being turned by a tug, rammed LCS 11 abaft the beam on the starboard side and did slight damage to our ship. I enjoyed going through the Panama Canal. The weather was beautiful, and to this day I am reminded of that place when I see soft, low, white, puffy clouds floating over rolling hills of very green foliage. We entered the Canal just after noon and were through at seven that evening. I had forgotten until I reviewed my notes that we went through the two sets of locks tied waist-to-waist with LCS 12. Another thing that made the canal passage interesting to me was that the small size of our ships put our decks level with the concrete sides. We could easily watch all the moves the canal workers made in managing the ships. Also, I remember being surprised to learn that the Pacific end of the canal is east of the Atlantic end.

The next morning we steered courses to the west and northwest going up the west coast of Mexico. I had the 0400-0800 watch and switched our AM voice radio to 1110. I was thrilled to hear the voice of Grady Cole on the WBT radio station in Charlotte, NC. That was a familiar sound to me and my family. Grady Cole was a popular announcer on early morning radio back home, and I couldn't wait to write Mama and tell her about hearing him that far away from home. After the war, I met him at the WBT station offices where I helped to keep details straight in the ballot count on the night of the November 1946 election returns.

December 1944 at San Diego

After our cruise up the west coast from the Panama Canal, our ship arrived at San Diego in early December. The records show that on December the 1st during the 1600 to 2000 watch crewman Duncan M. Baldwin came aboard. He is remembered for his drawings. He must have stayed aboard longer than the seven days indicated by the log. If not, he surely drew lots of pictures in that week because many of the shipmates remember him.

Sid Darion told me in a letter that Baldwin was somewhat older than most of us and described him: "I seem to remember he spent a lot of time in the radio shack. I also believe he was taken off the ship when he got ill. Anyway, Baldy—his hair was getting thin and he didn't care for that nickname— could draw quite well and, packrat that I am, I found some of his drawings in my mysterious box. I'm copying a few for you to see."

Baldwin's drawings

On December the 4th during the 2000 to 2400 watch,
our ship sent a message requesting that a doctor be sent
from LCS 17 to attend Charles Breese who was ill. At 2145
"a small boat belonging to LCS 17 moored to starboard side
of this vessel and Lt. (jg) Dickinson, MC, USNR, Division 15
Medical Officer, was received aboard this vessel to attend
sick man." I don't remember many sicknesses on our ship.
Our resident Doc Dobbs on the Eleven treated routine
medical problems among our crew, so Charles Breeze must
have had a serious problem.

On December 7, 1944, three years after the attack on
Pearl Harbor, LCS 11 was moored alongside LCS 14, port
side to LCS 17, at South Quay Wall, Berth 1, Naval Repair
Base, San Diego. At that base our ship was being prepared
for the voyage to Hawaii. The log shows that Warren C.
Eades signed every watch that day. At 0730 liberty expired
for the port section, my liberty section. No absentees are
reported in the log, but earlier liberties ashore had caused

some of the usual medical problems for members of the crew. These men reported to the U. S. Naval hospital for treatment.

We got underway from Repair Base mooring at San Diego on December 8th and sailed mostly 270 degrees, true, to the San Clemente Island area. En route we had deck court for two crewmen for being AOL (absent over leave). Kellog tells me that he is shocked when he looks at the log and sees how many men were frequently AOL, and I am surprised too. However, only a few of these absences were of a serious nature. Most were no more than 24 hours over due. We had several crew members transferred off LCS 11 just a few days before we sailed for Hawaii.

During the noon to 4 p.m. watch at San Nicholas Island we fired at a sleeve-target towed by a plane. I remember that a radio message came from the authority in charge of the operation. He said that if any more shells came close to the plane towing the target, as had just happened, the plane would return to the base immediately. I guess our gunners had trouble seeing that streamer fluttering behind the plane. I believe it was another LCS that frightened the pilot with those near misses.

On the morning of the 9th we made strafing runs on the beaches. I remember those big cloth targets set up at different elevations on the treeless hills. We could see tracers bouncing off the hills, reminding me of the sky-rocket fireworks fired by my Uncle Will Outen at Christmas time on his farm back in North Carolina. Our deck log records the firing of rockets on the beach, but I don't remember seeing that. Maybe I was in the radio shack since we were at general quarters.

We fired on a surface target and zig-zagged, but the biggest excitement came for the crew after four o'clock that afternoon. We anchored off the southern tip of San Nicholas Island in seven fathoms of water. It was still daylight. Some members of our crew decided to do some fishing. Sid Darion and Hoyle Gunter were the active anglers. Sid and another guy were always throwing a fishing line over the side when we anchored. At San Nicholas Island, they hooked fish almost immediately.

Within fifteen minutes almost all hands had fishing lines over the side. We caught a fine batch of fish—enough to feed the crew. I would like to know how many we caught and where the fishing lines came from so quickly. I suppose the fish were mostly Spanish mackerel. Some of the crew who were not normally cooks were involved in cleaning that mess of fish. I'm sure Hoyle Gunter, a North Carolina native with a cook rating, remembers this occasion because he would have been involved in cooking our catch. If I remember correctly, the fish were broiled and served for the evening meal the next day.

We were very busy with drills and exercises on December the 11th. The log says that during the morning the ship was involved in "tactical maneuvers and drills in the vicinity of San Nicholas Island." Among other things we laid smoke screens and conducted the following drills: collision drill, a fire and rescue drill, an abandon ship drill, hand-emergency steering, and a man overboard drill.

On December the 15th LCS 11 returned to the San Diego Naval Base. The morning log says the ship ran the degaussing range. This process involved de-magnetizing the ship. It is a procedure which helps to protect against mines that are triggered by close proximity to a magnetized vessel. The port watch had an overnight liberty. The log says Bill Herring was transferred off our ship.

On the 19th "All hands turned to for painting the hull." I must have slept through it as I don't remember a thing about it. The next day, Wednesday, we were towed out of dry dock and R. D. Walker reported aboard. On Friday, Emile Sprenger, SM 1/c came aboard, and on Saturday, the 23rd, Dobbs, Patenaude, Kupfer, and Balash missed roster at 0800. On Christmas eve, Sunday, I was added to the AOL list at the 0800 muster. My excuse was that Doc had me involved in an outing in Los Angeles, but I got back and reported in at 2300 that night. I didn't want to be late getting back to the ship—I didn't want to miss Santa Claus at midnight.

We had some memorable liberties while stationed at San Diego. Jack Kellogg of Council Bluff, Iowa, took many of the photographs of our outings. I have 136 pictures in one album, and they were all taken by Jack. But someone else took one of the photos of a liberty in Tiajuana, Mexico. It shows Kellogg on a donkey and G. O. Davis and me seated in a cart. We were all wearing sombreros and had *serapas* draped over our left shoulders.

Voyage from San Diego to Hawaii

On Christmas day, 1944, LCS 11 was moored "with port side to South Quay, Berth 2, US Naval Repair Base, San Diego, Calif." Santa Claus came some time during the night and left us a little gift from the USO. For each man there was a package containing a pack of needles, thread, toothbrush, toothpaste, maybe a pen of some kind, a shoe brush and shoe polish. These were good presents for us because we seldom spent our pay on these necessities.

It was my second Christmas away from home, and I felt the pangs of loneliness at not being part of the celebration down on the farm where I would have been helping my younger brothers enjoy their toys. But our crew was like a bunch of puppies: they didn't allow anyone to mope. They would pick at you, pull a trick, wrestle you, or tell some hilarious tale that you couldn't resist laughing at.

According to the 0400 to 0800 watch on Christmas day, John W. Balash and Ernest J. Patenaude reported aboard, AOL for 46 hours and 45 minutes. And during the next watch, Kupfer, Dobbs, Gunter, Davie, Fussell, Cavanaugh, Weir, and Zagara were listed as absentees. After five that afternoon, Cavanaugh reported aboard as 10 hours and 50 minutes AOL. For Christmas day dinner, we had a turkey dinner or maybe baked ham.

On Wednesday, December the 27th Captain's Mast was held at about noon and restrictions were handed out for all those guilty of being AOL. I got eight days restricted to the ship for my delay of 15 hours in returning to the ship. We knew in a few days we were pulling out for a battle zone and knew that could mean months of boredom in a space 158 feet long and 24 feet wide.

On December the 28th we moored at the fuel pier and at about noon completed fueling 21,504 gallons of fuel, making our draft 5 feet 6 inches forward and 6 feet 4 inches aft. We then moored along side LCS 58 at berth Number 1. That day, G. W. Reinas reported for duty. Then during the evening the following men reported back aboard for duty: W. W. Davie, H. Gunter, and D. D. Fussell.

On the 29th L. H. Gilliam reported aboard having been absent over leave for 1 hour and 40 minutes. We took on all kinds of ammunition, including 50 Very's cartridges, Mk red; 50 Very's Mk 2 green. These were signal flares. I think we had some of these on hand at Leyte, Philippines, to celebrate when word came that the Japanese had surrendered.

On the 30th we took food stuffs on board, including 1400 pounds of coffee, 700 pounds of sugar, 81 pounds of tomato paste, 42 pounds of raisins, 96 pounds of salmon, and many other items. Zagara was transferred off LCS 11 on orders of the dental office. Sprenger was transferred to LCS 12.

On January the 2nd, gunnery officer Ensign McCrea was detached from the ship and transferred to the US Naval Hospital with his baggage by order of the group medical officer, but by April 1, he was back on board. This transfer of officer McCrea was significant because when we reached Hawaii, Blair Vedder was assigned to LCS 11 as a gunnery officer to replace him. On January the 3rd just after midnight, Doc Dobbs returned from his 10 days and 17 hours and 30 minutes of AOL. All were present and accounted for at the 0400 to 0800 muster. At 1048 LCS 11 was being towed by a Navy tug boat. All ships in Berth 3 were moved simultaneously.

January the 4th was the big day for LCS 11, when we began our voyage to Pearl Harbor. We cast off lines and got underway at 1202. We were in company with LCS's 12, 13, 14, 15, 16, 17, 18, 19, and 44. I don't remember any destroyers sailing with us at the time. I suppose that at this late in the war, the Japanese had no submarines in the eastern Pacific.

I remember very well our sailing out that morning. As we came out of the San Diego harbor, some of our crew started singing, "Give me land, lots of land under starry skies above; don't fence me in." It was a popular song of the time. We were grinning like mules eating saw briars and were thrilled at the prospect of seeing Hawaii and a chance to beat up on the Japs.

Sacks of big onions and potatoes were lashed behind the deck house in the area of the aft twin-forty. One of the guys goaded me into joining him and others who were munching on big raw onions. We didn't have bread or salt to go with the onions. As we rolled along I began to get queasy. Up until now we had been cruising along following the coastline all the way from Boston. But now we were striking out over the world's largest ocean.

The log says our course was 250 true, but that seems south of a direct route to Hawaii from San Diego. Late in the afternoon that day we had a 33-minute general quarters. That was the beginning of the daily practice of going to general quarters at dawn and at dusk. We learned that these times of day were the most dangerous for an enemy attack by planes and submarines.

On January the 7th, our skipper, Lt. M. E. White, held captain's mast and deck court, assigning punishment for AOL cases. The next day clocks were changed half an hour. We also had a fire drill and small arms practice. The mechanics changed the oil in our two engines. On the 10th we had drill with a simulated direct hit by a 5-inch shell in the officers' wardroom and a fire in the number 1 crew's quarters and the ordnance storeroom. We knew that the real thing would have been plenty scary—especially a fire in the ordnance storeroom.

On January the 12th at 1747 radar man Tex Pace advised that we had made radar contact with land. At 1100 on the 13th we entered approaches to the Pearl Harbor Naval Base, and the crew gazed at the famous Diamond Head. An hour and a half later we had moored alongside LCS 17 at Berth T-12, Westlock, Pearl Harbor.

Solomon Islands, 1945

Our crew would probably agree that Hawaii was a beautiful place, but with so many Navy, Army, and other military personnel everywhere, I felt that I was on a military base anywhere I went. I did a lot of walking with shipmates on Honolulu. One time Kellogg and I went far up into the hills to visit Ralph and Mary Deal, a couple from Enochville, the village where I grew up. They attended the same church—Saint Enoch Lutheran. The Deals had gone to Hawaii to work during the war. They lived at 1519 A Alapoi Street, Honolulu, 6 T. H. Hawaii. Kellogg snapped some scenes from the Deals' front porch, which included Hickam Field and Pearl Harbor off in the distance. But the people who developed the film held it up until after the war because of military restrictions against photographing bases.

Another time Kellogg and I had with us John Sawyer, a radioman from LCS 12. We strolled under the palms down toward Diamond Head. I have snapshots of us taking turns posing with a gal there and cutting up on the streets. We sat on the "back porch" of the Royal Hawaiian Hotel, which the Navy had taken over as a place of rest and recreation for submarine sailors.

On January the 20th a dingy belonging to LCS 11 was hit by an 46-A Buffalo. A number of our crewmen were aboard the dingy which was several hundred yards away from the ship. Nobody was injured, but the boat suffered broken planks and ribs, and it sank. The log says that Raymond Reed, Charles Breese, Floyd Eaton, Adrian Perkins, Douglas Deschaine, and Paul Weir were aboard. Paul remembers that incident: "That buffalo was all steel, loaded with Marines who were on R&R and were bivouacked on the beach. Some of them ate aboard the Eleven because they were camping ashore. We hadn't had anything to drink as we were just heading for liberty. Our ship was anchored out in the back somewhere. As we came around a nest of LST's from one side, the buffalo came around also. They couldn't stop and neither could we, until we were standing on the bottom. I don't recall how we got the dingy back. They didn't stop, and we went after them, wet clothes and all. We were going to beat the hell out of them. We gathered up about 10 or 12 shipmates and went to take on the Marines. But since we were outnumbered, we put our tails between our legs and left the area. We did locate the crew that sank us, and they were the same fellows who were using the Eleven for a restaurant."

On January 23, 1945, LCS 11 was moored in our usual berth. The log says we started receiving electric power from LCS 12. Civilian workmen came aboard to install radio equipment. This is when we got our SCR radio installed. That radio had FM bands to use for voice transmissions. These workmen came aboard to work for several days.

On the 30th our ship took on ammunition, and the next day several 50-caliber machine guns were mounted in strategic places around the ship decks. They appeared to be an afterthought or a last minute plan to increase the ship's anti-aircraft armament. The Eleven was small. With three twin 40-mm mounts, four 20-mm mounts, and now several 50-caliber machine guns, she had a great deal of firepower for her size. Also incidental items were installed including "tool boxes and first aid boxes at all gun tubs."

On February the 2nd, we sailed from Pearl Harbor where we had been since January the 13th and set a course for the South Pacific. Other ships in our company were some that had sailed with us from San Diego. We were en route to the Solomon Islands for invasion practice.

Before leaving Hawaii, our ship was assigned another gunnery officer, Mr. Blair Vedder, to replace Mr McCrea who had been hospitalized in San Diego. In recent years Mr. Vedder explained in a letter to me how he happened to join our ship:

How I wound up on the 11 is probably very different in one respect from most of the others aboard, because instead of just being assigned to the ship, I pulled strings and went through a lot of shenanigans to get aboard. Actually, I wasn't aiming for the 11. I just wanted duty on an LCS in preference to the alternative the Navy almost handed me. Here's what happened:

I arrived at Pearl Harbor in the first week of January 1945, fresh out of Midshipman School along with a couple of hundred other "ninety-day wonders" and all with orders to report to AdComPhibsPac (the central amphibious command of the Pacific fleet) for assignment. Their plans for us were set; we were each to be given command of an LCM. That sounded very important until we found out what an LCM was and what it did. It was small; it carried one tank plus its crew or a couple of dozen Marines without a tank; it had two fifty-caliber machine guns for armament and would usually be in the first wave of an invasion. Worse yet, it was so small that it couldn't navigate the Pacific on its own bottom. It had to be carried around on the deck of an LST, and, at invasion time, be dumped unceremoniously into the drink and then loaded with its cargo. The word was, that the crews of the LCM were treated like the plague by their LST hosts.

It wasn't my idea of a glorious Naval career, and one night on a drinking binge with the personnel officer at the amphibious command, I told him how I felt and asked if there wasn't a better assignment somewhere. He said he'd look into it in the morning. We were both so canned that the next morning I was sure he would not remember the conversation.

To my surprise, he didn't forget, because when I reported in the next morning, he asked if I'd ever seen an LCS. I hadn't, so he described it to me. It sounded terrific, with its twin mounted forties, twenties, and rockets. Even its smaller weapons were the main armament on an LCM, and it would go where it was sent under its own power and on its own bottom. Then came the crusher: a group of LCS's were due at Pearl within the next week and one of them was short an officer who'd been hospitalized before the ship left San Diego. The trouble was that the ill man was the gunnery officer, and I knew —and the personnel officer knew— that I didn't know a thing about guns except what I'd read in the Midshipman School text books.

To this day I don't know why, but that personnel officer seemed determined to help me get aboard an LCS. He came up with an idea that damn near killed me but broke the impasse. The next day I was in a class of fifty officers and gunners mates at the Waianae Naval Gunnery School on the west coast of Oahu. The School was nothing more that a pressure cooker training and re-training center for the crew of ships engaged in anti-aircraft gunnery. It taught boneheads like me how the guns worked and how to use them. It taught the older hands the new modifications on the guns and the new tactics for using them.

Classes began at 0600 and concluded at 2100. Morning chow was at 0515 which was good because it was dark and you couldn't see what you were eating. From then on you were tearing down guns, putting them back together, and shooting at an endless parade of drones launched along the coast. It went on for two weeks (including weekends), and when it was over you got a certificate telling anyone interested that you were qualified to handle any of the Navy's latest anti-aircraft weapons from five inch/thirty eights to 50 calibers. The fact is that they threw so much at us in so short a time that I'm sure most of us forgot half or more of what we'd learned as soon as we walked out the gates of the school. I did, because it was brought home to me like a cold shower the day I reported aboard the LCS (L) (3) 11 as its new gunnery officer replacing Ensign William McCrea at the end of January.

When I reported aboard, I noticed a group of men standing around the forward twin mount forty. The barrels of the gun were elevated, and the recoil springs had been removed. "Good for them," I thought, "they're cleaning the weapon just the way we were taught to do it at Waianae." There wasn't time to watch them because the skipper wanted me below to fill out the mountain of forms connected with joining the ship. After a couple of hours in the wardroom and halfway through the stack of forms, there was a knock at the door. There stood GM 1/C Martin J. Francis well covered with sweat, grease, and oil. We introduced ourselves to each other and Marty said, "Mr. Vedder, we've run into a problem getting the forward twin mount back together, and wonder if you could come up on deck for a minute and show us what we're doing wrong." There was a twinkle in his eye which I took as a sign of friendship. I should have known better.

Two hours later and under the eyes of a couple of bored gunner's mates (but not Francis or the half dozen others who had been there at the beginning and who, I was sure, were back aft laughing their heads off), I still couldn't figure out why one of the recoil springs wouldn't go back on the gun the way we had been taught in gunnery school it should go back. When darkness came, the only help I got was from one of the crew who went to fetch a lantern so I could see. Incidentally, I think the skipper was in on this initiation because he'd walk by the gun tub every once in awhile and had not said a word.

Finally, in disgust, I announced that in the morning I'd get one of the specialists from Ordnance Depot to come aboard and fix the blankety-blank gun. With that, Marty Francis emerges out of the dark and scuffs around the floor of the gun tub which is littered with the gun's parts He reaches down and retrieves a small stainless steel pin from the pile. "I'll be damned," he says. "Who took this off the gun? It doesn't need to be taken off when you clean the thing." I was sure he was right because I'd never seen such a pin when we were cleaning identical guns at Waianae. Holding the pin up, Marty looked accusingly at the dozen men who had now re-grouped to watch the final act in the ceremony.

Locating a small hole in the base of the barrel, Marty inserted the pin and banged it home with a rawhide mallet. He then ordered his boys to put the recoil spring back on and this time the spring behaved just as I'd seen it behave a hundred times at gunnery school. "Thanks for your help, Mr. Vedder," said Marty. "Don't mention it, "I replied and staggered down below. There was an uproarious laughter on deck, but from that moment on Marty Francis and I got along beautifully through the rest of the war that we spent together. And I still think he was one of the best gunner's mates in the Navy. And that's how I happened to join the LCS (L) (3) 11, and I never regretted it.

On February the 9th LCS 11 and group crossed the equator. Our position was Latitude 00-00, Longitude 175 degrees and 40 minutes West. Upon crossing the equator, the old salts aboard initiated first-timers among the crew with an elaborate ceremony. Boatsun Mate Raymond V. Reed headed up the old-timers who began the initiation by clipping initials in the hair of each novice down to the scalp, indicating the sailor's home State. They were none too gentle in doing that. The fellows from Indiana, Illinois, and Iowa were easily marked with an "I" in their hair. But we from states like New York, New Jersey, and North

Carolina presented a problem, so our tormenters just cut a single letter, like "C" or "Y" or "J."

Donald E. Carlile of the MoMM division was dressed up as Neptunus Rex and sat on the after deck wearing his crown. His stomach was smeared with axle grease and other foul-smelling ingredients. We had to kneel in front of King Neptunus Rex and kiss his stomach. Any crewman who was reluctant got help from some old salts who shoved his face into the grease. I have certificates dated February the 10th with signatures of the old timers in charge of the ceremony. The first was signed by Sid Darion as Davy Jones and B. B. Vedder as Neptunus Rex. The second one was signed by R. V. Reed and J. L. MacLendon.

By February the 20th, our ship was moored at berth 15, Purvis Bay, Tulagi, in the Solomon Island group. We took on supplies and received mail. We lost no time in making some liberty excursions.

On February the 26th, George Robert Waldron, Everett LeRoy Terwilliger and Bernard Lyle Michaelson came on board. The first two became a part of ship's company. Michaelson worked as radioman on LCS 11, but he was a part of Division Staff under Lt. M. E. White. Later, when our skipper was promoted to Lt. Commander and took over Group 8, he moved to the LC (FF) 485. Michaelson reminded me that in order to continue in spirit as a part of Eleven's communication group, we established with him our own code and used our own frequencies to continue communicating with each other. He said that the Communications Crew on LCS 11 was "SAMPSON"; the ship Michaelson was on, LC(FF) 485 was "SHAKESPEAR"; and that our individual CW call signs were "SAIL" (Smith), "MAIL" (Michaelson), "HAIL" (Hammond), and "FAIL" (Faller).

We spent seven days on invasion tactics and mock attacks on the Islands. Many ships took part as we fired rockets and shot down coconut trees. On Saturday, March the 3rd, at Savo Island, we made a run on the beach, shooting the tops out of some palm trees. On March the 7th at about dusk we entered floating dry dock No.3 at

Carter City for some minor repairs and left dry dock the next morning at 0834.

I remember going from our anchorage to headquarters in the little town of Tulagi. A couple of us went in a small boat with one of our crew who was assigned to pick up mail. We crossed Iron Bottom Bay which was named by Ernie Pyle, where our PT boats and Japanese ships had battled in 1942-43. It lived up to its name because we could see quite a few of the sunken ships below us. Several cargo and fighting ships had been sunk, but the water was so shallow that parts of their super structure were sticking above water. During the time we were stationed in the Islands, several PT boats operated from their base on the bay. That day as we were crossing the bay, one PT boat came by us at top speed, and I expected our dingy to be swamped by the waves at any moment.

When we went ashore at the Tulagi, I noticed barefoot women who had a pad of skin on the bottom of their feet that seemed to be more than an inch thick, extending out along the edge of their feet. I assume this pad built up because they had never worn shoes. Some of the female natives did not have on bras, or anything else above the waist. I read in a Navy newspaper circulated in our area that a Navy chaplain had asked men aboard an aircraft carrier to donate T-shirts to the native women so they could cover up their breasts. The newspaper said the chaplain's staff gave the T-shirts to the women. But they just cut holes for their breasts to protrude through.

I remember the awful heat in the islands when we went ashore liberties. Here I decided tepid water from a lister bag wasn't as refreshing as an ice cold beer—my first beer. My mother had taught me and my brothers that drinking alcoholic beverages could be very detrimental to our health. She said that we might just fall over in a stupor after imbibing. And I had seen some of those drinkers around our little village of Enochville, North Carolina. Well, I did not want to become stupefied and fall down. At Fargo Building on Summer Street in Boston, several mates had offered to buy me a beer, and I always declined. This really challenged one guy who offered to pay me five dollars if I would drink a beer. Still I refused.

When we reached Panama and Mexico, Kellogg and some of the other crew members introduced me to rum and coke. I thought if it had something to do with coca-cola, it couldn't be bad or dangerous because lots of respectable people in Enochville drank cokes—or "dopes" as many of these old fellows called them. Well, it was hot as blue blazes there on Guadalcanal, and when we went ashore for recreation, I had a choice between drinking ice-cold beer or water out of a lister bag. I saw that when Charles Hammond, Jack Kellogg, Paul Weir, Scotty Rogers, or Doc Dobbs sipped on those beers, they raved about cold and delicious they were. I finally said, "Gimme a beer!"

One day several of us walked into the jungle near our anchorage. We followed an old trail to a small clearing where some logs had been felled across the trail. Stationed there were four Navy Shore Patrol men who wouldn't permit us to go farther. Beyond the barrier we faced dark-skinned natives. On our side were sailors. We looked at each other without saying much. I couldn't decide which was the zoo. Some guys traded belt buckles or belts and other things for shells and mementos. I was really impressed at how these natives scratched wherever it itched, shook their bare legs to shoo away bugs or flies and just casually looked us over. They were odd looking to us and we were to them, I guess. We looked back and forth at each other, as you might look at objects in an art gallery.

I gathered some small colorful sea shells along the coastline on one liberty, and I still have these in tiny boxes that our radio crystals came in. I remember a couple of us paddling our dingy up a little bayou until we were in a real jungle scene like the ones I had seen in Tarzan movies. The colorful birds on branches overhead were squawking just like the ones I'd seen in the movies. Suddenly a jungle shower came upon us, and we paddled furiously back to our ship. It could shower for 15 minutes and then suddenly the sun would be shining brightly. I decided this was a pretty place to visit, but it must be a very boring place to spend one's entire life.

I also remember seeing a big billboard among green trees on an island bluff that read: "KILL JAPS. KILL THE BASTARDS. Adm. Wm. Halsey."

It was about this time that Chuck Hammond, Robert Faller, and I decided that we should start keeping a record of our voice radio messages. We picked up a green-backed ledger book and settled on some rules we would use to determine what things we would record. Either Hammond or Faller printed this message on the inside cover of our new log book: "Voice Log—SCR" "Five cents a Peek. Payable First!!" "Log in all messages addressed to us or sent by us. Be sure to put time of receipt or time of transmission, and the date at the top of each page. Copy messages on scratch pad, break them down [to the essentials] and enter them in this [log]."

The three of us in the radio shack kept our log beginning about March 10th and continuing through late June when we left Okinawa and headed for Leyte Gulf. Most of our messages were something like the signalman's messages— facts concerning logistics, orders and tactical messages, commands received for making smoke screens, and pilots we picked up. Recorded in the log are lots of "shackle" and "unshackle" words in these messages, which means the letters and numbers between these words are in code and need to be looked up in the code book to determine their current meaning. We also had to look in the code book to determine code names for ships which changed from time to time.

On March the 12th we got underway in a formation going to Ulithi. When I left Tulagi, it would be 111 days before my feet touched dry land again at Leyte Gulf in the Philippines. Guard mail was passed to our ship quite a few times as we sailed toward Ulithi, and we passed it to LCS 14, LST 633, 762, 728, 949, 268, 772, 227 from LCI (FF) 1080. At 1225 on Wed. March the 22nd we dropped anchor at Ulithi Atoll.

Ulithi is a place of many small, widespread islands. On the horizon, near and far, many ships were visible. My notes say, "A mighty fleet is here—some British." We took on fuel from LCS 14, Oiler number 8, and we took on fresh water and other supplies. Mail was passed frequently—mostly Guard mail, or sailing instructions. The big moment we had been expecting came at 1525 on Sunday, March the 25th, when we started moving to form up on convoy at 1700. Our captain called a meeting of all men not on watch—especially division leaders—and told us we were going to invade Okinawa. That place was unknown to us.

Skies had been overcast all the time we were at Ulithi, and now we encountered rough seas and blowing rain. From time to time, we listened to Tokyo Rose on our radio. As we neared Okinawa, she told us we would not be successful in our efforts to invade the Ryukyu Islands. The weather worsened and we were informed by blinker light that shifting cargo on one of the LSTs had crushed a Marine. We were requested to lower our flag to half mast for 30 minutes during the burial-at-sea ceremony for this unfortunate Marine. With rough gloomy weather, a burial at sea, and only a few LSTs, LCS's, submarine chasers, and destroyers visible around us, we looked at each other and didn't feel so confident.

In another meeting of officers and petty officers on our ship, the captain made a talk and supplied information that included the topography of the invasion beaches, detailing the type of growth and gravel on them. Our communications officer, Ensign Frederick J. Henry, Jr., gave me a small booklet and discussed the names of ships which we should learn because they would be the ones most involved with us. He also told me to encode the call names of certain ships in the operation.

I went back to the radio shack and looked through the booklet of ships. It listed some 1400 ships in the operation—10 battleships, 20 carriers, many cruisers, hundreds of destroyers, and support vessels. I went out on deck and found the guys who had been worried. I flipped the pages of this little book and assured them this was one of the biggest invasion fleets in history.

THE BATTLE OF
OKINAWA BEGINS

In late March 1945 we were approaching Okinawa. On the 27th, we had an air alert and went to general quarters. That same afternoon we received "warning of storm bearing 052 true, distance 80 miles, velocity 80 MPH." But the storm gave us no trouble. In the midmorning of March the 29th a submarine contact was reported by a screening vessel.

Late in the afternoon, March the 31st, the day before Easter, I saw Okinawa for the first time. In the distance by twilight the island looked like a huge, bluish-gray whale. As we maneuvered closer, our ship made many changes in speed and course. Being new to battle conditions, I felt some apprehension. The rest of the crew were making wisecracks to conceal their nervousness. Everyone took a shower and put on clean clothes. I don't remember going to bed at all that night. In case someone might be sleeping, general quarters was sounded about 0200 Easter morning (and April Fool's Day). Stations were manned in record time. A ship in our group had been shelled, but the damage was slight. A short time later we secured from general quarters, and things seemed quiet in our area. But in the distance we could see flashes of gun fire.

After a good breakfast chow, we went to battle stations again. In the radio shack we began to look like ghosts, as we applied plenty of flash-burn ointment. Our faces and hands were plastered with the stuff. We looked like the walking dead as the pale red cabin lights reflected off this gray-greenish ointment. At dawn when the shooting began, we were back offshore not far from the bigger ships. Their big guns thundered and their shells sounded like express trains as they passed overhead. As we passed some of these ships, some of their crewmen gave us V-signs and waved to us.

From the radio traffic I could tell that some of the LCS's in other screening areas were having hair-raising experiences with suicide boats and small subs. Sad to say, some of our LCS's fired on one of our planes and shot it down. Now, the large ships passed the ball to us, and we moved forward to escort the landing craft to the beaches.

At 0755 we approached Yellow Beach No 1 with various courses and speeds. Over our radio came the voice of a flag radioman shouting to one LCS to move up on line and to another one, "You are too far ahead of the line." Then our ship laid down a heavy barrage on the beach. Our 40mm and 20mm guns were rattling for all they were worth. Then came the lunge and swish of the rocket barrage as all our rockets flew away to the beach. In our first approach to the beach, we fired 120 rockets, 1500 rounds of 40mm of various kinds including tracers. Then, abruptly, our guns fell silent. That meant that the first wave of Marines were landing.

By the time I was permitted to leave the radio shack and go out on deck, we were moving parallel to the shore, maybe a mile away. A pinkish-gray haze lay along the beach, and the sun looked like the moon when it is seen through a thin layer of clouds at night. There were plenty of ships in sight, but I wondered, "Where are the other ships involved in this campaign?" We did not seem to have the traffic jam that I had seen in photographs of the Normandy invasion. Later I learned that mock invasions off the southeast coast and the Kerama Retto operation west of Okinawa proper had involved many of our ships.

Our crew was quiet now. All of us were inactive except the few men who were reloading our rocket launchers. Then, with everything so quiet, word came down from the bridge that the Marines had landed. That meant our second barrage wouldn't be needed! I was pretty happy about that. We were through with our job for the present. Then we proceeded away from the beach a great distance, but even there I could see many of our ships. From that distance the beach was obscured by smoke. My cousin and dearly loved childhood friend, Ernest Outen was in the Sixth Marine Division. He may have landed on the beach that morning, but at that time I didn't know that he was involved in the Okinawa campaign. He was the oldest child of my Aunt Ruth Outen, one of my Dad's sisters. In 1931 Ernest and I started to school together in the same old three-room, wooden school my Dad and his mother attended. Usually we walked the two miles to and from school, but sometimes we could catch a ride with Ernest's father as he went to his job at Cannon Textile Mills.

That day at Okinawa, our ship was supposed to return to the beach to do salvage work, but thank God, there was nothing that needed salvaging. That's what Easter morning was like for us. At noon we had a sandwich. The rest of the day we kept congratulating ourselves, "Well, that turned out to be not so bad." In the evening our assignment was to protect our fleet against suicide boats and swimmers in the LCT area, Baker No. 1.

After the invasion on April the 1st, we began important but routine duties. On the 2nd our ship replenished fuel, water, and ammunition. We had a few air alerts and went in close to the beach again and learned that our ground forces were advancing very well. In Hagushi Bay we were assigned positions on the windward side of large ships—transports, communication ships, hospital ships, and other vessels—anchored there. Our purpose was to provide smoke with our generator to conceal these ships when enemy planes were reported heading our way. Other LCS's had been given radar picket duty around Okinawa.

Some were close to shore; others were as far as sixty miles out.

Bad weather set in on April the 4th. Radio messages to various ships included orders on how to deal with the weather: "Stop unloading. Get all landing craft off beaches. Take special precautions of dragging anchors. If necessary, ships get underway and keep clear of reef."

On April the 5th we patrolled in the vicinity of Point Bolo. That was a geographical reference point that enabled American forces to communicate to each other any location on or around Okinawa.

Point Bolo itself was a point on the northwest coast of Okinawa known only to the invading forces. Every location needing to be communicated was on a particular bearing from Point Bolo and a particular distance from it. On this day we were made to realize that the Japs did have some planes left. I heard plenty of war traffic over our radio that day. Sometimes ships reported victory and sometimes distress, as they put up a glorious fight. The Japs struck with more than a hundred aircraft, all divided into little groups of kamikaze planes. Five or six came into the anchorage and all were shot down, one falling near Admiral Turner's flagship and another near a hospital ship.

Our voice radio log shows other threats on the 5th. Early in the morning our destroyers and LCS's were told to "find and destroy all suicide boats and other possible targets." At 0348 I copied a message to Anzac from Cowhide 0: "Two-man submarine sighted in vicinity of Point Bolo." And later: "Anzac from Cowhide 0, Sub 3000 yards bearing 070 from Point Bolo. Course 170. Sub fired torpedo at Ribroast and torpedo exploded on reef. 0403Z."

The Japanese were counting on Okinawa to act as a bastion against the Allies. They wanted to keep us from acquiring a base from which to attack their homeland. The importance of these goals accounted for their determined, suicidal tactics during the battle for Okinawa. We saw their determination in the kamikaze attacks on our ships as we patrolled picket stations around Okinawa.

On April the 6th we went to general quarters five times. One time we were ordered to go to APA 129, but when we got to the designated area, the ship was gone. We were told to go to four other APAs, and they were gone, but we found LCS 12, 14, and other small ships. At 1613 off Blue Beach we fired on enemy planes and made a smoke screen. That smoke often covered the whole length of our little ship, and it was awful to have to breathe it.

On April the 7th, LCS 11 and LCS 13 were ordered to Radar Picket Station 12 (RP 12) sixty miles northwest of Point Bolo. About the time we arrived on station, we were ordered to return at top speed. We later learned this order was related to the final effort of Japan in a naval battle. In a determined effort the Japanese decided to sacrifice several capital ships and the brand new 69,100 ton Yamato battleship— the largest in the world— in a hopeless sortie toward Okinawa.

Japan had been building the Yamato for four years, and its military leaders decided it would be a disgrace for the battleship never to get into battle against the United States. But these Japanese ships were spotted coming out of ports, and our carrier planes began pounding them almost immediately.

Had we remained that far north, our 380 ton LCS 11 would have been in their path. The U. S. Naval command did not want LCS 11 and LCS 13 caught outgunned in that battle. I was really impressed with the battle line of U. S. ships we met outbound from Okinawa as we were returning to Hagushi Bay. Our ships were sent out to face the approaching Japs, but our carrier planes had defeated them before they came near Okinawa. This was the first big kamikaze operation against our forces there and was named "The Kikusui 1." The strategic purpose of Kikusui 1 had been to lure our ships and planes away from Okinawa proper so kamikaze planes would have a better chance of reaching our troop ships and forces on Okinawa.

Then for a while in all the excitement, our Naval officials must have forgotten about LCS's 11 and 13. I see evidence of it in our voice radio log. The code word for LCS 11 was "Dungeon 1" at this time, and "Highjinx" was the code name for the command ship. I notice that it was three days after we had returned to Hagushi from RP 12 before we were assigned new duties. In my handwriting in the log is this: "Dungeon 1 from Highjinx—OP—BT What is your present status and location.BT."

The answer to the command ship's question appears to be in Faller's handwriting as follows: "Highjinx v Dung. Reference your 092235Z We were ordered to return from RP Station 12 and remain 1500 yards outside of transport area on April 7 x We reported on return and have been given no further orders x Now located 2000 yards Green Beach No. 1 x TOD 092330Z." At this point Highjinx advised both LCS 11 and LCS 13 to proceed and report to a destroyer, DD-578, code-named "Cognac," for RP 12 duty.

Shooting Down a Val

We arrived at Radar Picket Station 12 in the afternoon of Tuesday, April the 10th, and we began our patrol with LCS 13 astern of the destroyer DD-578 code-named "Cognac." While patrolling, we followed a rectangular pattern either directly behind or off to one side of our lead destroyer. With its more powerful radar, the destroyer scanned the skies for incoming Japanese suicide planes. Our job was to act as fire support against kamikazes inbound from Japan who were seeking a target among the allied ships around Okinawa. Our armament against suicide planes was our 40mm, 20mm, and 50 caliber guns.

Destroyers could cruise at up to 33-35 knots. By contrast, an LCS could cruise at 18 knots if empty, but only around 15.5 knots when loaded. For that reason, some of the destroyer captains were rude to us, warning us to stay out of their way if they decided to go full steam ahead. So we followed along behind as best we could. But some of the destroyer captains would be quoted later as saying, "Even if the LCS's did not shoot down lots of kamikazes, they did a great service in rescuing sailors from the sea when our destroyers were sinking."

At 0850 the next morning, the 11th, our lead destroyer "Cognac" was relieved by DMS 27 whose code name was "Horse Thief." I think "DMS" was the designation of a series of newer destroyers that had been built with the added capability of serving as mine sweepers; thus "DMS" stood for "Destroyer-Mine Sweeper." The skipper of our DMS, "Horse thief," was a very knowledgeable and considerate man, judging from the exchange of messages recorded in our voice log.

Our ship, "Dungeon 1", and LCS 13, called "Dungeon 3" jockeyed for position around the larger ship. I thought LCS 11 was the ranking ship over LCS 13, but as we followed DMS 27, LCS 13 called our ship and said, "We have laid out a pattern for this patrol. Will you follow?" At that point "Horse thief," the destroyer-mine sweeper, came on the air and, as a way of settling the issue, said, "The patrol I gave is the one I intend to use. You may patrol as you wish. I felt my speed made it rough riding for you. That is the reason for the change. Do you understand?"

Our Radar Picket Station was approximately sixty miles northwest of Point Bolo. Quartermasters Jack Kellogg and Willis Rogers used a maneuvering-board paper to plot various ship movements. They furnished the radio shack with sheets of this graph paper so that we could plot distances to bogies. On this paper we laid out concentric circles around Point Bolo at 10 mile increments. We then drew similar circles around our own position so that we could instantly give Captain White the distances to bogies spotted around us. On one of these charts that I still have, the Point Bolo is marked with an X, and the location of bogies is indicated as "bearing 295 degrees, sixty miles from Point Bolo."

I notice now in the corner of this sheet of plotting paper that the price for a pad of fifty sheets was just 60 cents in the 1940's. It was an inexpensive but valuable tool for us. When I was recently visiting Curtis Dobbs in Opelika, Alabama, I told him that I still had a graph we used at Okinawa to plot the location of bogies. He asked for a copy and I sent him one.

On April the 11th we went to general quarters twice when incoming bogies were reported, but no enemy planes came within range of our guns. However, the next day our mettle was tested. In the early afternoon we went to general quarters, and within the hour a VAL Jap dive bomber appeared. It was in a steep descent high above us in what must have been a suicide dive. Both LCS 11 and DMS 27 began firing, and the VAL crashed into the ocean near the bigger ship.

Then a few minutes later another VAL appeared, making a low-level approach at us. LCS 11 began firing, and the plane veered over us passing from port to starboard, heading toward DMS 27. It was downed by our gunners as it passed over us and splashed into the water to our starboard side. About that event, Paul Weir says, "I can still picture that plane—we put three bursts in line behind it, and the fourth decked it! And all cheered."

We sent up a loud, tension-relieving cheer when the plane hit the water. It was as if our football team had made a touchdown in the last five seconds to win a Super Bowl game. I ran out from my radio station onto the main deck on the port side, opposite the galley, and I looked up at the 20mm gun tub on the upper level beside the wheel house. There was Ernest Patenaude scooping up empty 20mm hulls with a bucket and pouring them over the side, as calmly as if he did this job every day and was growing a little bored with it.

The rest of us were congratulating each other telling what we had seen from our different duty stations. Some of our crew speculated that the white cloth we had seen fluttering from the open cockpit of the VAL was a parachute, but I read later that a white scarf was carried by a kamikaze pilot as a part of his ceremonial garb.

About three in the afternoon, we were ordered to go to RP Station 14 to assist a disabled destroyer. We headed 020 true at 12.5 knots, and on the way, we fired on floating debris to sink it. About two hours later, we arrived at RP 14 but found nothing. Then we were ordered to go to another destroyer, DD-795, between RP 12 and RP 14.

At ten thirty that night we arrived at a disabled Navy PBM (seaplane) where we had been ordered to assist. It was unable to fly but could move along on water. It wanted to get back to its base and needed an escort. So about fifteen minutes later we got underway escorting this plane to Kerama Retto. Kellogg told me the PBM blinked over to us and asked us not to go too fast as the plane could only go 25 knots on the water. We blinked back telling him, not to worry, we could only go about 13 knots. We escorted the plane through the net gates between Aka and Zemami Islands in the Kerama Retto group at about three thirty the next morning.

It was daylight when we arrived back at RP 12. We were then assigned to a different destroyer, the Cowell, DD-547, with the code name "Sagebrush." During the remainder of the morning, we investigated floating objects, and picked up a life jacket. We went to general quarters a few times but did no shooting. Early that morning as crewmen on our ships had been having breakfast, we got a message relayed from far-off Washington, D.C.: "Attention! All hands! President Roosevelt is dead."

My mother and I wrote each other so many letters that we numbered the sequence on the outside of each envelope so we would read the letters in the proper order. That was necessary because aboard ship we usually got a bundle of letters at one time, after weeks of no mail at all. Our letters home were censored before they were sent to keep the enemy from learning anything important if they happened to intercept our mail. Because we knew that, one of my brothers and I cooked up a code before I left the States so I could tell my folks where I was. I used the first letter of every other word in the second sentence of the second paragraph when I wanted to give my location. I could use the first paragraph and the first sentence of the second paragraph to build up to a logical-looking sentence with the coded word. For instance, Okinawa was revealed in a sentence something like this: "Ola was kind and intelligent to notify Susie and Aunt Wilma about all that."

We also needed to keep information from our mothers at times. Paul Weir told me about his experience in that regard: "My mother always reminds me of the money I never sent home. My payroll was all screwed up for the longest time. After finally getting it straightened out, I was to the good about 6 or 7 hundred dollars. I made the mistake in one of my rare letters to tell her I would send it home. 'Watch for it,' I said. Well, I got into a card game with the big boys—Reed and I don't know who else. I took a hundred dollars to the mess hall, lost it, and returned to my locker and got the rest of it and blew it all. Mr. Reed and his men wiped me out. When I was done, I had to borrow a nickel to buy a pack of cigarettes. My mother never got that money. One thing I learned is never to play cards with the big boys. I haven't forgotten that to this day."

Sagebrush and the Ice Cream Incident

Often about dusk, in good weather, we sat on the gun tubs. If we did that in broad daylight, a message would likely come down from the con, saying we should find something to do. We talked about the day's events, or non-events, and wondered whether it was going to rain, much like the farmers did back home. Of course, the big difference was that farmers didn't worry about kamikazes, and sailors didn't worry about boll weevils.

On April 15, 1945, the destroyer DD-547, *Cowell*, code-named "Sagebrush," with LCS 11 and LCS 13 in support, was patrolling at Radar Picket Station 12 about sixty miles northwest of Okinawa. The Cowell's log entry for that day includes these words: "Delivered ice cream to the support craft LCS 11 and LCS 13 at daybreak."

According to our quartermaster Jack Kellogg who read the blinker message, Sagebrush had, indeed, made ice cream for us during the night and blinked to us to come alongside to pick it up. When Kellogg told me, I was delighted. We thought it was mighty fine of the destroyer's skipper to think of giving us this treat. And I began to imagine how good that ice cream was going to taste. Kellogg explained that we would not go alongside the destroyer until our captain had arisen about 0900. We sent that message back to the destroyer explaining our delay.

The news that we would get ice cream spread around the ship. LCS 11 was capable of making "ice milk" in a pan like layer-cake but not real ice cream that we had enjoyed in cones back home. As time passed, the craving for ice cream grew stronger in us. Finally Captain White came to the bridge and was told about the message offering us ice cream. Much to our chagrin, he ignored that issue and asked about other messages and conditions aboard the ship. I was told that when Sagebrush blinked another message to our ship about the ice cream, our skipper brushed the matter aside.

Some time later LCS 13 signaled us that they had picked up the ice cream from the destroyer for both LCS 11 and LCS 13. Jack Kellogg got Captain White's reply to be sent to the Thirteen. Kellogg said our skipper told him to tell them to "keep the ice cream." Well, we were crushed. I don't know how many men on our ship felt cheated by this news. But Kellogg and I felt that salt had been rubbed in our wounds when the LCS 13 signaled back later and said, "We are now eating your ice cream."

Kellogg sat down and penned a poem which was posted on the bulletin board after I typed it out.

This happened as we patrolled the China Sea.
The truth of the story can be proved by me.
We were on station there with a "Can,"
Whose skipper was a thoughtful man,
He imagined how good it would seem
To give the Eleven crew some ice cream.
His kind offer came to us by light,
And made the faces of our men so bright.
We never dreamed our skipper in his might
Would decline and be unwilling even to touch,
The ice cream we would have loved so much.
And now our days grow long and blue,
But men of the happy Thirteen's crew
Pass with broad smiles and eyes agleam
Because they ate the Eleven's ice cream.

Kellogg, forgive me if this is not quite the poem you wrote. You did a better job, but I think this is the essence of it. I recall that you kept me informed during the incident. Our skipper didn't have a palm tree we could throw over the side as was done in *Mister Roberts*. The best we could do was to place the poem on the crew's bulletin board for a few days. Lt. White demanded to know who wrote and posted the poem, but nobody ratted on you. It was great.

The poet was never discovered by the skipper, and Jack Kellogg is enjoying life in Council Bluffs, Iowa, to this very day. Mr. White, if you read this story, you can still court martial Kellogg, if you think he deserves it. The statute of limitations has not run out!

In 1988, I learned that the men of the Sagebrush were having a shipmates reunion, and I got in touch with Jacob "Jake" Jacobs, a crewman of DD-547 who was listed as the contact man. I wrote him a letter, telling him the story of the ice cream. He became very interested and checked the destroyer's logs which did show that ice cream was made for the two LCS's. He invited our entire crew to come to their reunion in Las Vegas that year, and he entered my letter into their ship's historical records.

Since I was leading radioman on our ship, one of my jobs was to set the watch schedules for the three radio operators. I was supposed to vary the schedule every two weeks, but Robert Faller of Saint Louis asked for the mid-watch—noon to 1600 and midnight to 0400—as a long-term schedule. Chuck Hammond of Louisville, Kentucky, asked for the 0800 to 1200 and 2000 to midnight. That left me with 0400 to 0800 and 1600 to 2000 watches. But because we all had assignments during general quarters, I rarely had an uninterrupted four hours of sleep following my watch because the Japs nearly always picked 8 am and 8 pm to send across some reconnaissance planes or raiders to pester us.

At 0830 on April the 16th bogies appeared, and a Combat Air Patrol was vectored to intercept. These American fighter planes flew regular patrols over the Radar Picket stations and the lead destroyer in a station had authority to direct the planes to certain targets. In this clash, two bogies were splashed, but one of our CAP planes was lost with the pilot bailing out. DD-547 started to rescue the pilot, but was ordered away to RP 14 to assist the destroyer *Hobson* which had been hit. For that reason, we were ordered to rescue the pilot and did. He was Marine Lt. John H. Peterson.

When the *Cowell* reached RP 14, she could not locate *Hobson* which had managed to steam southeast to pick up survivors of the sunken destroyer Pringle. So the situation was very fluid. The *Cowell* found a great deal of wreckage at the scene including papers, life jackets, and life rafts, but no survivors. It is possible that survivors had been picked up by other ships.

At 1150, on April the 18th, LCS 11 went alongside the *Cowell* to transfer the pilot Peterson whom we had picked up. On April the 22nd, LCS 11 was relieved by LCS 23 in that RP Station, so that we could return to Hagushi Bay and replenish our ship's supplies. On the 26th we were reassigned to a different destroyer at RP 1. Somehow, we didn't enjoy the same camaraderie with other destroyers that we had with DD-547 *Cowell.* Maybe one reason for the different spirit was that the top brass began to assign two or even three destroyers to each radar picket station. Also, additional LCS's and even LSM's were assigned to each picket station. As these ships completed duties in some other campaign, the command saw the opportunity to put even more guns where they could do the most good.

CLOSE CALL WITH A NATE

In April and May of 1945, LCS 11 continued patrolling the waters around Okinawa. The ship's history says we went to General Quarters 159 times for a total of 140 hours during the Okinawa campaign. I learned to cope with it. I just hung out in the Radio Shack as much as possible, so I only needed to put on my helmet and tighten my life jacket ties and slide into my position at the radios to be able to say: "Manned and ready."

One of the American ships lost at Okinawa was LCS 15. Radioman Harold Kaup was on that ship and described that event in a letter to me:

On April 22 about 1800 hours general quarters sounded. I remember dragging down the black-out cover on the porthole in the radio room when I arrived at my battle station at the voice radio. In the radio room that evening were Leo Renz, radio technician; Don Holden, radio operator; Dick Slama, RM, and myself. With us in the picket area was a destroyer and an LSM. Just as I finished dogging down the "black-out" cover, the "Can" called us on voice. The message was: "Watch out for the bogie coming out of the sun." I relayed this message to the Conn and immediately we opened fire. Even our 50 cal. were firing. Hearing the 50 calibers, I realized the bogie must be awfully close. So, for some reason, I put my helmet on. At that moment we were hit, losing power; and the radio room began filling with smoke. In the darkness,

I fumbled for the dog wrench; meanwhile someone had opened the hatch to the passageway. There were flames out there.

About that time I had succeeded in opening the porthole to get some fresh air and light. Looking out, I saw people in the water, and the deck on the starboard side directly beneath the porthole was already covered with water. By this time only Slama and I were left in the radio room as far as I could tell. I grabbed a battle lantern and shined it around to confirm we were the only two left. With that Slama started crawling out the porthole. I handed him his life jacket, then pitched mine out the porthole and proceeded to climb out after it. When I stepped down on the deck, the water was about crotch deep, and my life jacket was nowhere to be found. By this time the ship was listing badly to starboard with most of the fantail under water. The bow was clear of the water. I went over the side without a life jacket. Initially I clung to a 40mm ammo can. I am practically a non-swimmer, and finally someone helped me get to the wooden potato locker that was floating in the area.

The ship in the meantime started to turn clockwise with the fantail under water. She turned about 180 degrees and went down stern first. We were picked up shortly after by the Can and LSM. I ended up on the Can. The next morning, we buried our First Class cook at sea. Hammer was his name. I always thought that more than half of the crew was killed or wounded. On the morning of April 23rd the dead count was 15. Years later I visited our quartermaster, and he said he thought that 5 more perished, and a total of 40-plus qualified for the Purple Heart. Of the 4 people in the radio shack, Leo Kenz was lost; Holden, I believe, got burned going out through the fire, but his burns weren't serious, and Slama and I came through without any injury.

On April the 28th our ship was nearly hit during a kamikaze attack. In the mid afternoon, our captain had volunteered to take our ship in close to a jutting piece of real estate near the northern tip of Okinawa to rescue one of our pilots. When we approached the shore, we saw Japs running to a boat in an apparent attempt to get the pilot who, in his little bright-orange raft, was paddling toward us as hard as he could. We fired on the beach to give him cover, setting several dwellings along the beach on fire with tracers from our guns. A few minutes later we had the pilot aboard. He was Marine Lt. E. W. Langston from Monroe, Louisiana.

After picking up Lt. Langston at about five in the afternoon, we were steaming back to our picket station when we saw five dark specks low over the horizon several miles away. At about six thirty, we were on a Condition Blue alert, not the highest alert. The crew took turns going to chow, and when I came up to the fantail to put my meal scraps in the big barrel, I stood a while and watched those enemy planes in the evening sky some miles aft. Some of our crew remarked that the pilots were trying to decide whether to go ahead and die for the emperor or to prolong their lives a bit.

Because the shape of an LCS is similar to that of a destroyer, we speculated that some Kamikaze pilots may have thought our ship was a destroyer even though it was only one-third that size. It was a possibility when the enemy found us away from the larger ships without a means of comparison. After a time the planes split up and we saw one coming for us. Although it was almost seven in the evening, the sky was still light.

The story was that during this attack there was some confusion in the conning tower over who was to give the word to commence firing. I guess gunner John T. Lynn had already been removed from a gun mount. Otherwise he would have decided for himself. He was said to be quick on the trigger. The remaining gunners were a cool, disciplined bunch, so they waited patiently for the word. I have been told that as the plane neared, Captain White looked over at the gunnery officer and asked what he was waiting for. Or maybe it was the other way around.

When the command was given, I thought the radios would shake off the bulkheads in the radio shack. They had rubber mountings to save the tubes from such violent shaking. I could feel the vibrations of the ship and hear the roaring of our guns. I also felt the ship taking a hard left rudder. The maneuver was used by ships in battle to avoid an attack by enemy planes on the stern and to enable broad-side firing of the ship's guns. Evidently there were other Kamikazes nearby because our gunners were looking at other targets when this low-flying Nate came in just above the water.

Paul Weir told me in a letter what he recalled: "I can remember that plane very well. I was on the 50-caliber machine gun on the flag deck. That day as we were looking at other suicide planes, this devil came in on top of the water and no one saw him. The roving officer, I do believe it was Mr. McCrea, spotted him, came up behind me, and pointed me and the machine gun at him. Then the 20mm and twin 40mm turned on him, and before long all our guns that could were peppering away at this devil. He just kept on coming. He was close enough for us to see the spinner on the propeller, when the right hand—or starboard—wing went off. The plane veered off to port and crashed, sending gasoline and pieces flying onto our ship."

The Nate exploded about 30 yards off our port bow. Gunnery officer McCrea was overheard making the understatement, "That was close." I heard Knockabout Gilliam, the steward's mate, our only colored crewman, shouting as he ran down the passageway along the radio shack. In the radio shack, I thought he said we were on fire.

When I ran out the aft hatch near the galley, I could see a white wake where our ship had made the hard turn. Our chief bosun mate, Raymond V. Reed, was sitting on his butt at the 50-caliber machine gun by the forward side hatch. His legs were stretched forward and his hands were down on the deck at his sides. He was wearing a wide, toothy grin as if he was puzzled about something. Or maybe it was just a thankful grin that he had been spared. He had skinned his knuckles when the concussion from the exploding plane threw him to the deck.

Others were busy washing gasoline off the decks. Those of us who had been below wanted to get reports from the fellows who had been eyeball to eyeball with that Jap. There were plenty of pieces of the plane for everyone to have a few souvenirs. Soon the crew were passing the pieces around. Years later at one of our reunions, Woodrow Davie's son told me that his father had made bracelets and other trinkets from pieces of the plane.

There was lots of talk by the crew that night and the next day about our "close shave." I think it was especially tough on D. Keith Mong, who had had a cruiser sink beneath him. He knew how scary it could have turned out. But for the rest of us, we seemed to gain a veneer of invincibility from that close call.

During the attack, Lt. Langston, the Marine pilot we had rescued a few hours earlier, had been crouching behind our rear deck housing. When it was over, he emerged a shaken man and said to us, "My God, get me another airplane so I can get back up there where it's safe." Of course, this remark endeared him to us sailors. As we finished hosing down the ship and throwing plane parts into the sea, our Skipper White called Mr. Langston to the wardroom for some rum. Too bad he didn't have enough for the whole crew.

Late in the evening we were moved to Radar Picket Station 2. My notes say that a total of 105 Jap planes were shot down that day. Combat Air Patrol planes and ships of Radar Picket Station 1 got 17 planes. The destroyers in the RP stations were authorized to handle all messages to the CAP aircraft and to Point Bolo from which command ships coordinated the battle.

One night in May a few weeks later, the Japs sent a couple of Betty bombers to our area, and these planes flew back and forth, around over our station late at night for quite a long time, trying to provoke us into showing ourselves. Our ships ran in total darkness. Our people could see these planes flying back and forth like shadows silhouetted against the night sky. At that time guns weren't controlled by radar, and it was futile to fire at low-flying aircraft at night. So none of our ships were authorized to fire or show any lights.

We had recently had a new destroyer from another campaign assigned to our station, and its crew wasn't aware of how scary Radar Picket duty could be. On our radio I listened to the inexperienced radio operator on the destroyer fretting about being under attack, which was not true. He finally got so hysterical that officials on his ship removed him from the radio room. He had been calling to Point Bolo with pleas for help. A few unidentified radiomen on other ships had come on the network demanding that the guy get a grip on himself.

MAY 1945 AT OKINAWA

On May the 4th LCS 11 shot down another Nate and scored hits on a second one. We now felt like seasoned fighters. Reports said that a total of 40 planes were shot down around Okinawa that day. Radar Picket Station 2 got about 11. In addition to shooting down the Nate, LCS 11 picked up another American pilot, Lt. (jg) Chernoff who belonged to the carrier *Shangri-la*.

Early in the afternoon of May the 6th, Doc Dobbs and I were sitting and talking on the 20mm gun tub just outside the hatch door aft. It was a fine day with bright sunshine and puffs of cumulus clouds here and there. There were three LCSs and a destroyer patrolling the station north of Okinawa and in sight of Ihebya Shima. We were expecting just another day of routine and false alarms. We did have F4Us or Corsairs flying Combat Air Patrols almost continually during daylight hours. Our leading destroyer had a group of such planes under its command. Dobbs and I glanced at these planes from time to time. Suddenly we saw a puff of reddish-black flame and smoke. Since we weren't at general quarters, it was surprising. But we realized we had seen an aircraft being hit.

About this time we went to general quarters. Our skipper had volunteered to attempt the rescue of a downed American pilot, and our ship was ordered to go close to the island Yuron Shima off the northern tip of Okinawa where the plane had been hit. As we approached the Island, we could see flames on the shore as other CAP planes strafed grass-covered huts. We realized that we were at risk of being sunk by fire from shore batteries. Our ship fired some 20mm and 40mm rounds into the area. But we had to get close to shore, and it was a job for an LCS with its shallow draft.

In the distance we could see the pilot in his small orange raft, like a pea in a pod. Since we were at general quarters, I was in the radio shack but was able to peek toward shore at times when the zig-zag maneuvering offered me a chance. I could see men running along the shore about two miles away. The planes kept strafing the shore to suppress any firing at the downed flier. After some tense minutes, we had the pilot, Major Ed F. Cameron, USMC, aboard. He was the fourth pilot we had rescued.

On May the 7th ships on Radar Picket duty were re-assigned to different stations. Our station was eliminated because the Army radar on the northern point of Okinawa was able to take over duties that had belonged to picket ships. We returned to Hagushi Beach anchorage where LCS 11 turned over to AGC 11 the pilots Chernoff and Cameron that we still had aboard. On the 8th we received this message: "Germany has surrendered unconditionally to Western Allies and Russia. Surrender took place at General Eisenhower's command post. Surrender was signed by General Yodel, German Chief of Staff."

The period of May 8th, 9th, and 10th was used to replenish stores and make engine repairs. On the 8th we sent a message to *Cutthroat,* the command ship, saying, "We require one carburetor and oil strainer complete for Hale pump type Tare-one-one-eight Chrysler Industrial Engine."

About log keeping, *Cutthroat* sent this message: "All lobsters (LCS's) this area. Submit immediately rough draft of any action. Any planes splashed. This for future action also. In smooth form put any outstanding action by crew members in accordance PAC Flt letter 301-44 and ships come along side and deliver report whenever in anchorage area. *Cortez 2* and *Cortez 5* designated ships to deliver reports for units when ready."

About maintenance work done, LCS 11 reported to *Cutthroat*: "Work accomplished 3 days maintenance period. Heads on engines removed, air intake parts cleaned. Pistons, rings and valves inspected. 3 heads replaced. 20 valves replaced. Engines synchronized. We are ready for sea."

On May the 11th, LCS 11 took part in the invasion of Tori Shima. The reason for this operation was to set up a radar station on this small island and to destroy a suspected outpost that was sending information to incoming Jap planes. During the assault, we saw a couple of amphibious tanks sink as they approached the shore. Late in the evening, when we started back to Hagushi Bay, our group of ships was attacked by enemy aircraft. The flight of planes came into view about five miles away, low in the sky on our starboard stern.

Dewey Fussell on the forward 40mm mount was ordered by Mr. White to fire on the planes. He tried to explain that the forward gun was blocked so that it could not be pointed in that direction because it would be aiming at our conning tower. At this point our skipper banged Fussell on the helmet for refusing to obey an order. After being told he was under arrest, Fussell was sent below.

It was a sad incident because our captain would not drop the issue. The nearest General Court Martial sat in Guam, and finally the captain was dissuaded from taking that drastic step. So a lesser court was eventually held at which the charge against Fussell amounted to little. Meanwhile other ships in our group behind our ship had shot down three of the planes as we headed into Hagushi Bay about twilight.

On the night of May the 14th we were on Skunk Patrol. The term "skunk" meant a Japanese suicide boat. These craft were designed to run into the hull of our ships and explode. There were also swimmer suicide attempts on our ships. Because these threats were greatest in Allied ship anchorages like Hagushi Harbor, we regularly patrolled these waters at night. That midnight we chased a blip on our radar screen. I remember the excitement and shouting as we sped about in the dark. It was a tense operation because those suicide boats were reported to have many pounds of explosives in their bows. Suddenly, the ship lifted up in the water and came to a scratching halt. We knew we were grounded on a reef. Different members of the crew were blamed for that mishap—radar men and others. And Captain White thought some of the crew blamed him.

The engines were reversed and revved up very high but to no avail. Next we pumped out our water supply. Then we pumped out some fuel, but still she didn't budge. Then all hands were called forward to empty the magazines and carry the ammunition aft. When this was done, the ship was down by the stern and was listing to the starboard side, but she would not come off the reef. I recall the rocking and pounding of the surf against the ship through the morning hours as the tide went out. Not many of us got any sleep that night. We knew our ship was a sitting duck if we were spotted by the enemy.

By dawn the ship was listing at an awkward angle. About that time an L-5 scout plane made some passes over us. It was a high-winged plane like a Cub. The side panel of the cockpit was lowered and the two guys shouted some questions at us as they banked around overhead. I thought it was interesting that they wore red baseball caps as if they were out on a picnic excursion. When the tide came back in that morning we were towed off the reef by a tug boat.

But soon we discovered that our ship was damaged. We reported, "We are afloat now but have several holes in bottom." At first, the command didn't take our report of damage seriously. At mid-morning LCS-11 was given orders for another night on anti-skunk patrol "on a line north of anchorages. Be alert for skunks and swimmers."

At about eleven that morning I sent this message: "*Rocket* V *Dungeon 1* . . . Our hull is buckled under engine room.

There is possibility shafts are out of line. Do not consider it advisable to stay underway. Advise." Rocket then assigned LCS 89 to take the duties we had been assigned. And we were reassigned to the task of providing smoke coverage for large ships in the Dodger area. On the 16th we went into LSD 7, a floating dry dock, for repairs. We came out of dry dock on May the 20th.

LCS 11 and crew in dry dock

While we were in dry dock Woodrow W. Davie was given permission to leave the LCS 11 and travel to Okinawa to see his brother who was a Marine fighting there. Davie was an unforgettable character. He was always complaining about our situation, duties, and chow. But his eyes twinkled even while he was griping, and we could tell that he was enjoying himself. What follows is Woodrow's account of his trip to visit his brother on the Okinawa.

Woodrow hitched a ride in a light observation plane. It took him to a point near the front. His brother was on the front lines down toward Naha, an area that was not very secure. He was able to find his brother, but when night came, the people in charge put Woodrow in an old hut. They gave him a 45 pistol and told him that no one but the enemy was to the south of him and that if he heard anything outside of his hut in that direction during the night, he was to shoot first and ask questions later.

Needless to say, he didn't sleep much under those circumstances. By this time he was beginning to yearn for the white sheets on his bunk back on the Eleven. After spending a sleepless night in the most primitive conditions, he was ready to head back to his ship.

The problem was that there wasn't a scout plane around to fly him back to the beach. He started out walking and observing all the filth and destruction along the way. As he walked the rutted road, a command car came along going his way. It was one of those topless four-door cars with big tires being driven by a marine, and it had two Jap prisoners sitting in the back. The driver stopped and asked Davie whether he wanted a ride. Davie was tired of walking and accepted the offer.

"You'll have to hold my carbine on the Japs while I drive," the Marine told Woodrow, who reluctantly agreed. Off they went down the road which had bloated corpses of the enemy lying here and there along its edges. Davie soon noticed that the Marine made little effort to avoid hitting the bodies with the vehicle. Woodrow said the stench was something terrible.

When he arrived back at the ship, Davie told us about the K-rations, the stench, the lack of bathroom facilities, the lack of a decent place to sleep, and all the physical hardships endured by men ashore in the battle areas. A few of us listened to his story and were certain that we had heard the last of Davie's bitching about life aboard LCS 11. But the next day he strolled down the port side aft and said, "Damn! Horse crap for lunch again!" We nodded knowingly and said, "Griping Davie has recovered." He was an actor, but he never learned to hide the grin that always crept out during his tales of misery.

An Unlikely Meeting
at Okinawa

My Cousin Cecil Jones, son of my mother's sister, grew up around Clearwater, Florida. He is one year older than I am. He was born on April 8, 1924, and I was born on April 8, 1925. He joined the Navy about 1941 when he was seventeen and became a member of the crew of the *USS North Carolina* soon afterward. He was a quartermaster on that ship when the Japanese attacked Pearl Harbor. His rating put him on the bridge of that ship where he was often at the helm under the direction of the ship's navigator, Commander Thaddeus J. Van Metre.

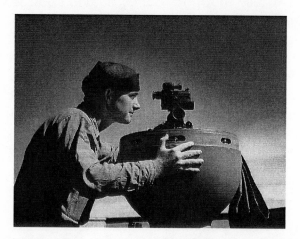

Cecil Jones on the USS North Carolina

The *Carolina,* nicknamed "The Show Boat," was seriously damaged only once during the War. That was during the Battle of Guadalcanal in the fall of 1942. Cecil tells me that the aircraft carriers *Wasp* and *Hornet* were within sight of the *Carolina* at the time. One of his shipmates ran into his quarters where he was sleeping and said, "The *Wasp* has been hit by a torpedo." A few seconds later the *Carolina* was also struck by a torpedo. Both weapons had been launched from the same Japanese submarine.

The damage to the *Carolina* was on the forward port side. Nineteen compartments were flooded and eight crewmen were killed. After undergoing some temporary repairs, the battleship steamed several days at about 18 knots to reach Pearl Harbor where the damaged hull plating was replaced. But more work on the battleship was needed. One propeller shaft was bent out of alignment, and that couldn't be fixed at Pearl Harbor, so she sailed to the Navy shipyard at Bremerton, Washington, where the work could be done.

Since promotions were likely to be slow among quartermasters aboard the *Carolina,* Cecil asked to be transferred to another ship. He went to Astoria, Oregon, where the *USS Meriwether* was being finished and served aboard that ship during her sea trials. He then sailed in the *Meriwether* back to Pearl Harbor where he was assigned to the *USS Teton,* a vessel fitted out as a command ship. The *Teton* was built on a freighter hull and bristled with radio antennas. Since it coordinated communications during sea battles, many of the crew were radiomen. In the spring of 1945, the *Teton* was in the waters off the coast of Okinawa.

By that time, I was in the Navy on LCS 11 and was also at Okinawa. On the *Teton,* Cecil had been promoted to Chief Quartermaster on April 1st— the same day that the Battle of Okinawa began. He didn't have a proper uniform that morning and appeared in the Chiefs Mess hall wearing a hat and dungarees. He said a Marine master sergeant befriended him and made him feel welcome there.

The *Teton*, was code-named "Delegate" in its role in the Okinawa campaign. Our ship was in Hagushi Bay on May the 12th when I looked out and saw the *Teton* at anchor a couple hundred yards away. I knew that my cousin was on that ship and *asked one of the signal men* on our ship to send a message to Cecil on the *Teton*, suggesting that he and I meet and talk a while. Cecil thought it was a good idea and approached his navigator, Lt. Commander W. D. Smith, told him about me being on the nearby ship, and said we hadn't seen each other in several years. Cecil requested that he be allowed to come over to LCS-11 to see me.

"Are you nuts?" Commander Smith replied, "We're in the middle of a battle here!" But he went to the Executive Officer with the request that Cecil be allowed to take the LCVP (a small launch) over to my ship. The Executive Officer said it would be okay. Commander Smith went back to my cousin and said, "Okay, Jones, go over for twenty minutes. Stay on the fantail—in sight—don't go below. And when you get a signal to come back, be quick about it!" A couple of sailors from the *Teton* brought Cecil to the Eleven in the launch and then stood off a short distance in the boat until he was ready to return.

We hardly knew where to start to catch up on family news. We figured how long it had been since Cecil came up from Florida to visit us on the farm at Enochville. It had been six years. He said he was very thankful that the war was over in Europe where our Uncle Julian was serving in the Army. He said he was afraid our Uncle would get wounded or worse before the fighting ended. Julian was the brother of my mother and Cecil's mother and was already in his forties. Then by signal light Cecil was ordered back to the *Teton*. We shook hands, and he said, "Let's get this war over and get home. Rita and I will have to come up to old N. C. then. Lawrence, take care of yourself." He climbed down into the launch. Later, he told me that he had to chase his ship down because it had started to move to a different location.

Cecil Jones and Lawrence Smith, 1987

When I wrote a letter to my mother that night, I told her, "Just about 10 hours ago I shook hands with Cecil Jones. You can guess how we covered 6 years in 10 minutes. It had been almost 6 years since I saw Cecil last—when he was visiting us then, I accidentally stepped on a nail, and he took me to the doctor."

In 1987 Cecil wrote me a letter in which he said:

History books call it "the Greatest Sea-Air Battle in History" and you were there. It started at 4:00 PM on Easter Sunday, April 1, 1945. I was promoted to Chief Quarter-Master at 12:01 AM and had my first meal in the Chief's Mess that morning. It was also the "Last Battle" of World War II.

I went in on "D" day [first day of battle] and stayed until +72 [first day of battle plus 72 days]. During this time we recorded 99 air raids. It was the greatest naval armada in history. Forty carriers, 18 battleships, 200 destroyers, hundreds of transports, cruisers, supply ships, net layers, submarines, minesweepers, gunboats, LCS's, landing craft, patrol vessels, salvage ships, & repair vessels. 1,321 ships transporting 183,000 assault troops. The Japs lost 110,000 dead. The U. S. lost 12,281 dead of which 5,000 were U. S. Navy. I was 21 & you were 20 seven days after "D" day. Well, Lawrence, that was 42 years ago, and it seems like a lifetime. My seeing you that day was one of the highlights of World War II. It was one chance in a million. Love, Cecil

Record of Picket Ships
at Okinawa

Landing Craft Support (Large) No. 11, (LCS 11) would be dubbed "THE LUCKY ELEVEN," by her crew. Looking at the statistics of the Battle of Okinawa, below, one can see why we feel extremely fortunate that we came through it unscathed.

The following short article appeared in *TIME* magazine on July 9, 1945:

"BATTLE OF THE SEA: The Little Ships":

The Navy last week totaled up its losses off Okinawa; 4,907 men killed or missing; 4,824 wounded—nearly 20 percent of its total casualties in all oceans for the entire war. Okinawa was also the war's costliest operation for ships, according to the Navy's own figures; 33 ships sunk, more than 50 damaged.

One of the big reasons for this damage was finally passed by censors. The gallant little ships (Destroyers, Destroyer Escorts, and LCS's) which formed the 'Picket' line 25 to 50 miles above the main anchorage had been severely mauled. By staying out front, the little ships with thin hulls had been able to warn the big transports and gunnery ships of approaching Jap planes, but they became the first Okinawan targets in the sights of the Japanese suicide planes, and they took the greatest concentrated damage, plus more than 1,000 casualties.

But the little ships stuck to their picket lines and their men stuck to their guns. They set the world's anti-aircraft record by shooting down 490 planes during the 82 day battle. They went to general quarters 150 times. The picket-line men's spirit was set down for history in a message sent by one little ship (LCS) in April . . . "Have been hit by two suicide planes, shot down a third, and am taking damaged destroyer in tow."

The *Sacred Warriors* by Denis Warner and Peggy Warner with Commander Sadao Seno, and *A Glorious Way to Die* by Russell Spur, are two books that give lots of insight into the matter of kamikaze attacks. On the first page of the first book is this statement:

On radar picket duty to the north of Okinawa, the Twiggs and other destroyers had LCS's as support ships. "They were good to have along," said Lt. Pederson, "if for no other reason than that they might still be afloat to pick up our survivors . . . All during April you had to consider yourself very, very lucky to come through a suicide attack."

In reports of the DD Aaron Ward sinking, her skipper said: "Dead and wounded filled all available spaces, and men fought fires with seawater and buckets. Others loaded the wounded on to life rafts and tied them alongside so they would not drift off. And then along came the 'crummy, dirty, lovely little LCS 83' to take off the wounded."

Ships involved in the fighting received the following message toward the end of the Okinawa battle:

From: Commander Task Force 51

To: Task Force51

This dispatch is for the purpose of giving special honor to the ships who are and have been on radar picket duty. DD's, DE's, LSM's and LCS's, repeat LCS's, are on this distant guard whose work is doing so much to help our troops make this operation a success. We are very proud of the magnificent courage and effectiveness with which these vessels have discharged their difficult and hazardous tasks.

A second message followed:

From: Commander in Chief Pacific Fleet:

We share with the entire Navy the admiration expressed by CTF 51 for valor and gallantry of the resolute ships on radar picket duty who are contributing so magnificently to the successes being achieved by the current campaign.

Many other events occurred on our tour of duty that will linger in the memory of our crew as long as we live. On June the 25th following the Battle of Okinawa, we were ordered to proceed to Leyte in the Philippines to prepare for an invasion of Japan. On July the 1st my liberty section went ashore. That was the first time we had set foot on dry land since March one hundred and eleven days earlier. We had been penned up in an area 158 feet by 24 feet. We got to know each other pretty well. We learned to work together and to depend on each other, and in the process some memorable friendships were created.

Fortunately, the Japanese surrendered, but we were destined to face another great danger. En route to Aomori, Japan, in September, 1945, our little ship was tossed about by a furious typhoon. At recent reunions, members of our crew have agreed that our riding out the typhoon was more scary than the Japanese suicide planes.

Typhoon at Okinawa, September 1945

LCS 15 was one of the ships sunk during the Battle of Okinawa. According to the reports we had, it was operating in a Radar Picket Station when it was struck by a Kamikaze plane. The plane crashed against the bulkhead outside the passageway beside the radio shack, buckling the bulkhead It was impossible for radiomen in the shack to get out except by climbing through a porthole on the other side. It was reported that a radioman lost his life because he was too large to squeeze through the porthole. I have a letter from a survivor of the LCS 15 sinking, radioman Harold Kaup, who gives an account of the attack but does not say that anyone died because he couldn't get through the porthole.

Be that as it may, when the story about the crewman on LCS 15 reached us, we began to think about our porthole as a possible avenue of escape from the radio shack. Our radio crew was made up of Robert Faller, Charles Hammond, and me. Also in the shack were radar man Tex Pace and technician Sid Darion. We all tried our skill at getting through our porthole. Faller immediately went on a diet and practiced getting through that port hole several times, a very reasonable thing to do. Fortunately, there was a ladder strapped underneath the 20mm gun deck right outside our porthole. Most of us could reach out and grab the rungs of that ladder and pull ourselves through rather easily.

After the battle of Okinawa had subsided and before the atomic bombs were dropped on Japan, American forces gathered in the Philippines to plan for the invasion of Japan. We went to Leyte about June the 10th and were involved in the staging. But we also took recreational trips ashore.

Beer was made available by the Navy to sailors who went on liberty in the islands. As a way of regulating the amount of beer we could drink, Mr. White and other skippers issued chits which limited the number of beers a group of sailors from a ship could have. A leader was authorized by the chit (signed by the skipper) to get beer for his group. Some of the leaders of these groups would come in the radio shack and ask the radiomen to type up a beer chit for LCS 15. We would copy one just like our skipper had signed, and different ones of us would sign a name for the LCS 15 skipper. That way some of our crew were able to drink the beer for both LCS 11 and LCS 15.

I don't believe the people on shore ever caught our crew members doing this. Because 15 had sunk, it was not listed on the reference sheet they used, and our guys would mumble something like, "I swear. We get cheated every which way. We risk our behinds on radar stations at Okinawa, then they fail to list our ship on the beer sheets." By that time, the poor shore people had tears in their eyes and said, "Okay, go ahead this time, but I've gotta check this out." On the next trip, different people would be on duty, and our guys would go through the same routine again. I think Sid Darion may have been the ring leader who masterminded this ruse.

Mr. White was strict, but on at least one occasion he stood up for a member of his crew. G. O. Davis says, *I remember one day when part of the crew was coming back from liberty, and a fight broke out between them and the crew from LCS 14 on an LCVP. Junior Dennis was about to get belted when Captain White put his arms around the other man who then called White an S. O. B. So White decked him. I believe that was one of the few times White stuck up for his own men.*

Junior Dennis had some loyal friends in our crew. Sid Darion remembers the same occasion that Davis tells about, but adds a few details about John Belcastro, another member of our crew. Sid said, *Belcastro did have a temper. I remember a liberty boat coming back to the ship from a recreation area with a lot of very drunk sailors aboard. There had been a beauty of a free-for-all on the liberty boat, and someone from another ship had slugged Junior Dennis. Steamer White was on the boat too, and I saw him slug a sailor from another ship who badmouthed him and tried to swing at him.*

Sid goes on, *When the liberty boat got alongside the 11, Belcastro, who hadn't even been on liberty, heard what had happened to Junior and leaped from the deck of our ship onto the liberty boat and started to pound the guy who hit Dennis. There was a Captain's Mast later. Steamer White complimented Blackie (Belcastro) for his spirit and support of his shipmate . . . and restricted him to quarters for a number of days for fighting!*

Sid also tells of a quarrel that broke out aboard ship between John Belcastro and Richard Choike: *One vivid memory that comes back was a real argument between Choike and Belcastro. I can't remember what it was about, but it almost got physical, and you remember Choike was a lot bigger than Blackie. Well, Blackie looked Choike straight in the eye and said something like, "Where I come from we don't get pushed around. You may take me in a straight fight, but I never forget. You'll go on liberty and something will fall on your head in an alley. We'll get into rough seas and someone will help you over the side. Just don't mess with me." Belcastro meant every word of it, and the reason that it sticks in my memory is that Choike obviously believed him. The two became very good friends after that.*

In early September 1945, after the War was over, LCS 11 was sailing from Leyte in the Philippines toward Tokyo Bay to join other forces in the occupation work in Japan when we got warning of an approaching typhoon. We were many miles south of Okinawa, but we were told to head for Buckner Bay and the safety it offered. This Bay was on the East side of Okinawa and was large enough for many of our huge ships.

We were nearing Okinawa when we received an update on the storm and how we should deal with it. I don't know exactly how many miles we were from the safety of the bay, but we had a terrible night ahead of us. Then by radio we were told to veer away from that haven at Buckner Bay because the storm was so fierce there that cruisers and large supply ships were dragging anchor. These ships were being sent out to sea to battle the typhoon on their own because of the damage occurring to ships inside the bay.

We soon began to feel the full effects of the storm. That would scare me to death now, but then I somehow felt that God would protect us, and our crew would handle the ship safely. With all the hatches locked down and the air vents shut, we weren't getting fresh air as usual. In this situation the atmosphere in the ship had a strange and suffocating effect.

A little before dark, I went outside the hatch that opened off the galley where the ladder went down to the mess hall-sleeping quarters. Safety lines had been strung everywhere outside for men to hold onto so they would not be blown or washed overboard. To walk anywhere, inside or outside, was like being a circus performer walking on a big ball. It was a balancing act to keep from being thrown against a bulkhead. In the radio shack we held to the bulkhead stanchions or whatever was handy.

When I looked aft, I saw a hill of water that looked sixty feet high, and I was scared. Since I had no business outside, I went back in so I wouldn't see the huge waves— much higher than our ship— rolling toward us. As these waves lifted the stern of the ship, the bow went down at a terrible angle, like a submarine making a crash dive. The screws came out of the water at these times, making a zizzing sound, as they revved up faster in the air. I found that I could hear that zizzing sound inside the ship in any compartment.

Back inside, I went into the passageway that ran along the port side of the radio shack from forward quarters to the galley. Four or five men were crouched near the door at the galley. They explained that if the ship capsized, they felt they had a fighting chance of escaping to the open sea by being so near the door. I didn't know whether I should join them or not, but trying to sleep was difficult. To avoid being thrown out of the sack, I had to put my heels down between my mattress and the pipe that was the outside rim of my hammock. And I had to brace myself in the bunk with both arms. I was amazed that sixty-six men and six officers were going about their business of either trying to ignore the typhoon or—if they were on duty— trying to uphold the traditions of good seamanship to keep us afloat.

In 1991 Gunnery Officer Blair Vedder commented in a letter to shipmates that the brief entries in the ship's official log are misleading. Part of the reason, he said, is that the logs were written "several days, and in some cases, several weeks after the fact."

It's too bad because, as the reader will discover, the finished logs are sterile. They give none of the color and flavor of the events they record. They omit far more than they tell. For example, the entries for September 16-17, 1945, only hint at the fact that on those days the ship was in the midst of the most vicious typhoon to strike that part of the Pacific in many years. The log entry for September 16th speaks of 'high winds and heavy seas.' It neglects to mention that the wind velocity was in excess of 70 miles an hour and the seas were estimated by aircraft carriers in the vicinity to be running in excess of 60 feet from trough to crest, with some of the 'growlers' approaching 80 feet. On that day, several small ships turned turtle when they broached in these seas. The LCS 11 almost broached as she attempted to round the south coast of Okinawa to seek shelter in Buckner Bay. The log fails to mention that this is why she changed course suddenly from 080 degrees to 180 degrees at 10:30 that night.

I saw our shipmate, Murray, from Upper Darby, Pennsylvania, come up from his sleeping quarters and go to the head. He was rubbing his eyes with one hand as he held onto the railing with the other. One of the guys at the hatch, watching and waiting for the ship to capsize, said, "Murray, how the hell do you sleep through a typhoon?" Murray said, "Ah, I always say my prayers before I go to bed."

I must have slept some, and as daylight came, I was thankful to note we were still afloat and the waves were down to 10-12 feet. Our skipper had kept our ship from broaching. Ernest Hayes and Floyd Eaton manned the helm during the worst part of the storm. We had traveled at 5-10 knots—whatever speed best balanced our ship to the size and frequency of the waves—and it had worked. We heard later that several cruisers lost large portions of their bows. Apparently the bigger ships with their long water lines were under more stress. The long ships had taken several cruel waves at once in the towel-wringing episode. Captain White tells me, "What I remember from the vantage point of the Conning Tower was that when our ship was at the bottom of a wave trough and the ship ahead was also at (or near) the bottom of a trough, it was not visible to us. The ship ahead was about 250 yards distance. Our mast height (and theirs) was about 65 feet. These typhoon waves were exceedingly high and very long. The length was to our advantage in that we never hit one wave until the previous wave had passed our stern. Thus larger ships broke up while we remained in tact."

It was cloudy—completely overcast—and the wind was still strong enough to blow spray off the tops of the waves. Our quartermasters were unable to shoot the sun to fix our position. We estimated that we were southwest of Okinawa. The skipper came into the radio shack to see if we were hearing ships talking on our SCR radio. We could hear traffic but it was sporadic, and we weren't able to get much useful information from it.

Some hours passed, and I was able to learn that we were listening to traffic at Guam. When I told the skipper this, he pointed out that we were 1500 miles from Guam and our SCR radio was not supposed to send signals that far. We attributed this phenomenal transmission distance to the disturbed atmospheric conditions caused by the storm. Later in the day we were able to contact other ships and determine our position and resume our course to Tokyo Bay.

Walter L. Cameron, Jr., was our executive officer during the typhoon. In a letter to me he said he had served in the European theatre and "took an LCT into Normandy on June 6, 1944." After thirty days of leave in early 1945 he was assigned to LCS 11 and went to Pearl Harbor.

I eventually caught up with you in the Philippines shortly after you got there from Okinawa and relieved your namesake, T. A. Smith. At some later date I relieved M. E. White and took over command in the fall of 1945, eventually bringing the ship LCS 11 back to San Francisco in May of 1946.

Lt. Cameron continues, *Among other things, I remember the Pescadores" where LCS 11 had mine sweeping duties. "It was night when we came in, and we had to tie up alongside another ship already moored to a buoy in the harbor. The wind was fierce (they had called off our mine sweeping operation in the China Sea because of the weather) and the ship we had to go alongside was swinging in a 180 degree arc. That turned out to be one of the most difficult ship-handling jobs I had ever faced, but we got it done without smashing up either ship. The next day there was a very short liberty.*

The thing that I remember most, however, was the number of men in that stalwart crew who in a very few days thereafter came down with a certain unmentionable disease. I wonder to this day how that could happen, given the short time anybody was ashore.

Sid Darion responds to Mr. Cameron's observation: "As to how anyone could come down with certain unmentionable diseases in so short a time, well, I know it might have happened to more of us if it had not been so difficult to win the favors of the young ladies."

We'd been at sea for quite a while and were our normal horny selves. The strange problem, as I remember it, was that the women our group contacted would not cooperate for money or candy bars. They wanted T-shirts! It was t-shirts or nothing, and Scotty and I decided we didn't want to go back to the ship out of uniform. So, perhaps Navy regulations saved the two of us from a fate worse than . . . I'm referring, of course, to our Pescadores visit.

My Letter from Aomori, Japan

Aomori Wan, Northern Honshu, Japan, September 30, 1945

Dear Folks,

I want to tell you some of my experiences and opinions about the occupation of Japan in progress now. We are anchored in a bay just off the city of Aomori. The city has a population of 93,000 as recorded by a chart I was looking at several days ago.

We arrived in this area on the 24th of September. The next day we made our landings at Aomori without any kind of opposition. From the sea we could not tell how thoroughly the port had been damaged . We could see with binoculars two tankers sunk at their piers and one other type of ship sunk. We knew that our bombers had been at work here. Over in the Bay of Ominato I saw a Japanese cruiser and a destroyer with the majority of their sterns under water— more work of our bombers. I know that it was bombers because it would have been suicide to have come through the straits and down this beautifully-shaped bay in war ships.

Yesterday morning at 0800 a small boat came by our ship and picked up a sight-seeing party. I was in that party. As we neared the beach, I thought about how many Marines and sailors and soldiers had approached the enemy beach like this, but with more apprehension, I am sure. As we neared the beach, we saw a crudely painted sign that struck us as funny. On the concrete wall was written: "THE SEABEES WELCOME THE US ARMY 9-22-45." In other words, the Seabees had preceded other American units by 3 days. I guess key men were placed ashore at different places as soon as possible after the V-J Day signing.

Then I looked for Japanese. They were there all right. And I couldn't help but remark to one of my pals, as we stepped onto Japanese soil, "These are the Japanese that were going to march down the streets of New York and Washington."

As we went ashore there was a feeling of apprehension at first, but that soon passed. As we walked down the streets, we felt confident and proud. And I must say we should all be proud of every war bond we bought. I surely am. Where the uptown section used to be there are only acres of rubble and little piles of tin and metal that the Japanese have gathered together. In every pile I could see there was a smashed bicycle. There were no walls remaining like you see in the pictures of bombings in Europe. But occasionally there were a few vaults standing. I had read how our pilots had bombed industrial sections of Japanese cities and hadn't bombed their churches and schools. I had half-way believed it. Now I know that it is true. I saw amidst all the rubble a shrine. The grounds around it were clean. Even grass grew along the walks. The trees on the borders of the grounds had been singed, the only damage done. This shrine only covered an acre, probably less. I saw four school buildings. A few windows had been blown out; all the walls were standing.

Now I will give you a few of the rules of our going ashore. Every group of men must have an officer with it. Nothing was explained to us, but we were told that officially there was to be no trading with the Japanese. It is a difficult situation. If we traded, it would put them on an equal basis, and soon their discipline would become lax. If we took things without trading, it would be looting. And that is what the Japanese would do if they invaded our land. It is the same fraternization problem in Germany . . . We planned to trade or do something to get some souvenirs.

No one in our crowd had any sort of weapon, besides a few knives. I thought this unusual. In pictures, I had noted that everyone seemed to be wearing a side arm in Germany, and here we were in the most treacherous of countries and none of us carried a gun. We never needed one.

We walked through the streets that had been cleared. Some new wood houses were going up. But they would be more like a garage to us. Some of the Japanese were beating out smooth scrap tin into bundles. From outward appearances there is plenty of clothing, but no one wearing shoes except soldiers, among the Japanese. There were plenty of Japanese dressed as soldiers.

Our group entered a school house. There were rooms that had adults in them looking busy like they were carrying on the city government or something. They had arm bands that said PREFECTURE GOVERNMENT. We looked at the posters on the walls, written in Japanese. We went up stairs and saw the children's classes in the yard back of the school. Adults crowded the hallway. They stayed out of our way. Some of the older Japanese took off their hats and bowed. A few younger ones had a slight look of contempt. One thing very noticeable was the Japanese policeman's uniform. Admiral Nimitz could take lessons—the epaulets on their shoulders had designs and stars in yellow gold.

We went into one room in which there was only one man. The desks were small and crude. We looked through their class books and other equipment. In a corner was a baby grand piano. The boys found it to be locked. The Japanese never protested against anything we did, but they surely looked on closely. After some gesturing we managed to get someone to unlock the piano. One of our fellows began to play boogie woogie. The Japanese from up and down the hall gathered around. Some smiled, others looked fearful.

The fellows were patting their feet and gesturing with their hands, and the piano was roaring. I am sure the residents wondered what was happening.

After a couple of tunes we went out the back way. We stopped where the kids were sitting at their desks in the yard. We stopped and Charles A. Dubois took out some candy. Our guys broke the candy up and threw it in their midst. That is when the school class was forgotten. They charged like a bunch of cattle. But one of them spotted an old Japanese coming out of the school house and with a little rattle, rattle sound, warned the others, and they remembered their seats. The teacher with a half smile came up and talked to the youngsters who looked sheepish and slunk down in their seats. Our officers arrived about this time. They happened to be the most carefree that we have and enjoyed everything as much as we did.

The squealing kids had brought all the Japanese to the windows in the school house. My pal got a book that had pictures of Japanese bombers bombing American warships. But the pictures were drawn, not photographs. Another drawing showed Japanese soldiers charging a beach, running over an American flag.

Soon we came to the area that had been untouched by bombs. We crossed a railroad which apparently had been untouched. The streets between the closely jumbled houses were fairly crowded with bicycles, carts, and rubber-tired taxis drawn by horses. Here we had a chance to see many examples of how the Japanese reacted to our presence. Some looked curious, but all seemed to go about with the air of business as usual. The older men and women bowed. One cigarette is worth about 50 cents here. It was really comical the way some of our fellows did the Japanese. One had something wrapped up. One of our fellows would look at it hard, and the Japanese man would bow and unwrap it. He would smile and bow when the fellow shook his head negatively and walk on. But about this time another of our fellows would come along and stare at the object and the Japanese man would unwrap it again. I guess he thought we were inspectors. The people wear everything imaginable for shoes. The women were wearing traditional dress.

Some of the kids were pathetic. And an American soon feels kind-hearted toward them. The kids would steal their mother's household belongings and trade them for candy. Also some of the grown-ups traded with our fellows. They were quickly learning that the Americans can't hold a grudge. They bestow a very charming smile upon us when we give their children some candy. We became quite disgusted with one of our fellows. I guess he thought we came here to give the Japanese relief. I guess he has already forgotten the suicide planes that came at us and about our friends who have been killed on the lonely islands of the Pacific. This fellow took candy and cigarettes and handed his out like the Red Cross . . . .

On our arrival back at the beach, we saw that some Japanese were working for the U. S. Army and probably getting good pay. Their job was giving boxes a shove on a roller chain. Well, I guess this is enough of my observations of what is going on around here.

Lawrence

Two Castaways at Aomori, Japan

On September 24, 1945, in company with LCS Group 9 and other U. S. Navy ships, LCS 11 arrived at Ominato, Japan, en route to Aomori for landings to carry out the occupation of the country. The next day's landing was carried out without any untoward incidents.

On September the 30th, a group of LCS 11 sailors went ashore, unarmed, as a liberty group. I remember some of us gave chocolate bars to the few Japanese kids brave enough to approach the rambling sailors. This was the first time I had stepped ashore on Japan, and I looked in awe at the clutter of burned tin roofing piled in heaps where small houses had previously stood.

That evening LCS 11 joined several other LCS's tied alongside a large cargo ship. By this time LCS 11 and the others had movie projectors of their own, and as darkness fell, movies were being shown on the fantails of several ships. Another LCS 11 crewman and I could not decide which movie we wanted to watch. We could easily step from one LCS to another across the narrow space between them. We kept going across the LCS's until we went aboard a big cargo ship. There we found a movie being shown on a large screen. We liked the movie and took a seat.

At one point during the movie, I noticed that one of the LCS's was pulling away from between the big ship we were on and where I supposed LCS 11 was, about five ships away. I was unconcerned and turned back to watch the rest of movie we were enjoying. When the movie ended, my buddy and I went down the gangplank to the first LCS and proceeded across the other ships toward our LCS 11 on the outside. But she was not there. I went to the radio shack of the LCS we were on and asked a radioman to call Dungeon One and advise them of our circumstances. In reply, we were told that LCS 11 was having difficulty maneuvering because one engine was not operating, and it would anchor nearby and pick us up in the morning.

I don't recall who my LCS 11 buddy was who had become marooned with me. I thought for forty-two years it was Jack Kellogg, but he denies it. Anyway, my buddy wondered where we would sleep. We were on LCS 17 and one of their radiomen came up with a good idea. He said since he was on duty, I could use his bunk. When his relief came on duty, he said he would go to his relief's bunk. The same arrangement was worked for my buddy from LCS 11. He made arrangements with the appropriate crewman in his rating. We had no change of clothes, no toothbrush, and no shaving gear, but we were treated royally by our new-found shipmates. When morning came, LCS 11 was still not in sight. By radio we were told that it had gone to some distant location to refuel and get a part for one of its engines. Well, this sort of thing went on for three days. I think some of the guys on LCS 17 even let us borrow a change of clothes while ours were washed.

After the Battle of Okinawa had slacked off in June, many picket ships including LCS 11 had been sent to Leyte Gulf in the Philippines to await the assault on the Japanese mainland. While we were anchored in the Philippines among hundreds of other ships, some daring radioman on one of those ships started playing music over his ship's radio. He was conducting a regular radio station on the voice network that all the ships monitored. As a result, an officer had come on the air and warned the culprit broadcasting radio music that ships with radio direction finders were prowling the gulf and that the offender would be found. He said the guilty sailor would be given the full weight of Naval punishment when he was caught. But, so far as anybody knew, the sailor-turned-disc-jockey was never found.

I took one look around the LCS 17 radio shack, and I was sure I was aboard the ship that had in its radio crew the guy who had been broadcasting music on the ship's radio back at Leyte Gulf. The radio shack had those huge records that were as large as a tin tub, with Bob Hope programs on them, Tommy Dorsey, and you name it. These huge discs were called V-Records and were made for Armed Forces Radio programs. I saw that this shack had various radio hook-ups to other compartments aboard the ship and special microphones. When I asked the leading radioman whether he was the "ghost radio station," of Leyte Gulf fame, he just grinned.

Well, after three long days we managed to get back aboard the LCS 11 and at 10 p.m. on October the 6th we got underway for Yokosuka. Evidently Robert Faller and Charles Hammond and the other radiomen on our ship had covered very well for me as I do not remember getting a reprimand. From Aomori LCS 11 went on to Yokohama, Yokosuka, and Sasebo, and Shanghai.

The final part of this story played out after I was a civilian. I returned to civilian life on April 15, 1946, hoping to get into journalism. But colleges were bulging at the seams with returning veterans and I could not get into the University of North Carolina, but I did attend a temporary division in the evening at Charlotte College. My brother Jack was at Lenoir-Rhyne College in Hickory at the time studying for the Lutheran ministry. He pulled some strings and I enrolled there on June 14, 1947.

I went through college, finishing in January 1950. While I was a student, I did freelance features for the *Hickory Daily Record*. Upon graduating, I became a full-fledged reporter for the paper. One day the sports editor left to take a job on the *Greensboro Daily News,* and his old job was shoved on me. I liked to play sandlot baseball and pitch horseshoes, but I was just a mediocre sports fan. Still, with the help of others, I dug in.

One assignment in that work as a reporter led to an exciting remembrance of my days in the Navy. When Lenoir-Rhyne College hired a new basketball coach, Jim (Pappy) Hamilton, in June of 1950, I was asked to cover the story. Some sports-minded Hickory citizens had hosted a dinner for the new coach at the Hickory Country Club on June 13th, and the newspaper sent me to the dinner.

After the formal part of the program was over, I had a chance to talk with Coach Hamilton and to ask him a few questions. As we talked, I learned he had been in the Navy. He said he had been the captain of LCS 17. I was amazed. So just five years after being an uninvited guest aboard his ship for three days, here I was eating steak with the skipper. Since I was no longer in any danger of being reprimanded or thrown into the brig, I told him the little story about my three-day visit aboard his ship at Aomori, Japan. I asked him whether he had heard that two sailors from LCS 11 had become stranded on his ship.

To be truthful, I was quite chagrined by his answer to my question. Coach Hamilton said he "thought maybe he remembered some incident like the one I described." That was all he had to say about it. The next time I get marooned on somebody's ship I am going to kick the radio shack apart, so even the captain will know I was aboard.

My Letter from Yokohama, Japan

Yokohama, Japan, October 15, 1945

Dear Jackie,

On October the 9th LCS 11 arrived at Yokosuka Naval Base, just south of Yokohama and a bit further south of Tokyo. We arrived at just the right time, for a typhoon was brewing. We found a secure berth, which was fairly easy as Yokosuka is a very large base stretching to Tokyo. As you probably read in the papers, the storm damage was considerable at Okinawa.

On October the 10th I went on liberty to the city of Yokosuka. On the way there, I saw a Japanese cruiser and three destroyers. The only Japanese battle wagon still afloat was near our ship. The weather was rainy and muddy on the 10th. We were not allowed to take more than two packs of cigarettes ashore. Shore Patrol men attempted to see that no more than that were taken. A pack easily brings 20 yen. That is $1.30 in our money. A dollar is equal to 15 yen. Only Japanese money is any good to you here. The sailors and soldiers get their pay in Japanese money.

Yokosuka was the most modernized place we had touched since leaving Honolulu. The buildings looked fairly nice. Only one small square of this town was hit or destroyed. Here the Japanese have open shops, and if you have the yen you can buy whatever they offer. There was nothing in the food line, but there were a few trinkets like those you might see in the Dime Store at home. But they are more expensive here. The shops are little cubbyholes. Barbershops are open for business. Also I saw a "Wotch" (the way they spell it) shop and a photographer shop.

And, of course, there were plenty of Japanese. They are all very small, and I have to stoop down to enter most doors. Everywhere one hears the clip-clop sound of the wood pieces that they use for shoes. Otherwise the natives appear well clothed.

There was a noticeable increase in the number of Japanese who could speak English here. I noticed that our Navy had requisitioned the best buildings for administration purposes. We saw Japanese trucks and cars driving on the "wrong" side of the road.

There was at least one prospering Geisha House. A very, very long line of servicemen waited to enter the house. The line wound around corners and along the streets. My pal and I stood beside the line near the front, where it turned into a courtyard and a building. Then we saw men leave the building and go across a bricked yard to a building three stories tall. We talked to a couple of fellows coming out of the second building, and they told us service was pretty good except for the fact that the guys had to kneel down on bamboo mats which cut the "hell outa' your knees." However, the price was right—10 yen or 66 and two-thirds cents.

I saw several buildings that looked like theaters, but they are now closed. As I have already said, I saw very few bomb-damaged places around Yokosuka. I guess things are about the same as before the war except that the Japanese are now working for the Americans.

A fairly nice place has been set up as the Enlisted Men's Club, but so far the most attractive thing about it is the serving of beer. They do have some shows once in a while—a couple on Sunday. If I were a collector and could look far enough ahead, and had a locker to store them in,

I might get fans or dolls or some such souvenirs. Would you believe that the movie we saw the night before we got underway for Yokohama was "Destination Tokyo."

On the short trip to Yokohama, I noticed many more of our ships. As far as I know the *New Jersey* is our newest completed battleship, and it is here and a very beautiful piece of workmanship. After seeing Okinawa and Leyte, I am used to seeing a harbor of about 500 to 1000 ships anchored about. A very short distance from us, there are two Japanese ships that had been under construction, but were never equipped. One is an aircraft carrier and the other apparently a transport. The British have a very nice sized token force here. Also I have seen some Australians.

On October the 14th I started out on liberty in Yokohama. It was the clearest day we have had in a long time. Immediately we saw that the B-29s had done a job here. However, the docks and waterfront seemed undamaged. This is the first time since Tugali (in mid March) that we have tied up along a pier. I just looked out the porthole and saw land; that seems strange. I can't explain how or why, but there are certain burned out areas and then a building standing almost untouched. I saw frames which used to be freight cars, now hulks, but still on the tracks.

We thumbed a ride in a jeep with a Lt. Colonel in the Army. We rode a couple of miles, and the scenery was about the same. We caught a ride back in an Army truck. We saw an electric train that went pretty fast over an undamaged bridge or raised railway 2 or 3 miles long.

One home with a concrete fence around the front had a nice metal plate at the gate with the inscription "Yamotochita." But the once elaborate home appeared collapsed from within. After a while we came to "Church of the Sacred Heart." We continued along this route. My pal wanted to turn off, but I was always interested in seeing what was over the next hill. Soon the street narrowed, and we turned down some steep steps. Water was running over them. Rich grass and weeds were growing there. At the bottom of the steps, we came out into a thickly populated territory, and I was nervous because the Japanese looked at us like we were the first Naval personnel to come this far from the water.

Apparently some English was spoken here, for hordes of kids hollered "Hello, Hello," and when we said "Goodbye," they took up that in chorus, only cutting their syllables shorter. Once a middle-aged man, in a startled manner, said: "Hello there, my friends, how are you?" I wondered how long we had been his friend.

We saw a crowd and found some sailors were selling a few packs of cigarettes. I don't think food would have gathered a more interested crowd. Selling cigarettes at $1.30 per pack, a person could get rich if he had paid only 5 cents per pack for them. The Japanese tried to sell us old photos from their family albums.

Soon we were in a crowd that made us think of Norfolk or San Diego days. We saw American military personnel—nurses, and others.—dressed in nice clothes. I might add that we were dressed up in our real liberty uniforms—the first time since Hawaii. Maybe the next port will be Tokyo, or better still, just any old port in the USA.

Lawrence

My Letter from Sasebo, Japan

Sasebo, Kyushu, Western Japan, November 7, 1945

Dear Folks,

Premier Suzukua says that 10,000 Japanese will die this winter from disease and starvation. In Yokosuka and Yokohama, cigarettes bring 20 yen per pack. In Tokyo they bring 30 yen. That is $2.00. If any people have to have their cigarettes, it is the Japanese. I think they would almost starve for a smoke. They very unashamedly pick up the butts that Americans throw down.

From October the 13th to October the 24th, we were moored to North Pier, Yokohama. Many Japanese were working with lumber that was piled nearby. Every day when we ate chow, they would gather around near the stern of our ship and shake heads and motion and try to get everything left on our trays. After the first day, they brought cans and held them out. No matter how mixed up everything was, they ate it all with equal relish. One of our cooks makes his soup quite hot with pepper. One Jap guzzled down a bunch before he tasted it. He choked and sputtered around for a while. All this caused some arguments among our crew. Some would give to the Japanese and others would not. Our boys broke out a can of lemon drops, which cost probably 10 cents. The Japanese were willing to pay 50 yen per piece.

When I went on liberty to Yokohama, there was nothing to be bought to eat, and we were advised to take our water along. After my pal learned he had a good friend in the Army stationed there in Yokohama, we would always go to the Army camp to eat noon chow. Some Japanese hang out for food at a bombed-out block downtown,.

Can you imagine going down town and not finding any stores with foodstuffs in them? But you would quickly notice that all the Japanese look really healthy. I believe they are not actually starving as much as they are just hungry for a different diet. They like our food because it is a variety compared to what they have been having all through the war. They can be seen eating some rice or potatoes but nothing else that I have recognized.

One evening one of our guys told me that a Japanese boy was outside and that he was cute. I went out there and two of the fellows were learning Japanese and teaching him English. Our guys would point at their chin and ear and different objects and the boy would say them in Japanese. He seemed very intelligent. He was 11 years old. To demonstrate sleep, he would lay his head over on his folded hands. When we wanted to teach him a word, he would lean very close and watch our lips as we pronounced a word. Soon we were pointing to different fellows and getting him to say their names.

They had given him some food in a can. He would eat big mouthfuls of this and then talk some more. When some officers came along, he folded his knees over his can and looked very unconcerned and innocent. After they had passed, he said, "MPs." We found that he knew some English all right. He said he had a brother in the Kamikaze. He said that his brother went "zoom and boom into a ship." He spread out his hands to demonstrate a big explosion. He also informed us that all this happened at Okinawa. The guys rather smiled at this, thinking maybe he didn't really hit a ship.

I am sure that the American occupation will change the customs of Japan. The Japanese men pay their women no respect. Their women occupy about the same plane of living as the Indian squaws are reported to have occupied in the early days of our history. You never see a Japanese woman and man walk down the street side by side.

General Eichelberger is in charge at Yokohama. On the front of the building that is his headquarters is a sign showing an embarrassed GI talking to a Japanese woman and the wording under the sign says: "Learn Japanese at our night classes." In the *Yank Magazine* published in Tokyo, McArthur is quoted as saying there will be no rules restricting fraternization between GI's and Japanese. He says there is no better way of enlightening the people in the ways of democracy. It also reported that Japanese girls are eager to learn the western dances so they can participate in USO dances and Red Cross programs planned for this winter in Tokyo and Yokohama. I think the Japanese women view the Americans with a courteous curiosity. The Japanese men could be said to view us with indifference. The children like us. If you give one or two kids chewing gum, you soon are a Pied Piper of old.

I don't know who started the G. I. Joe name, but it really sticks. All the children in the Philippines and Japan call us "Joe." And if they can speak no other English, they can speak "Gum, Joe?" "Candy, Joe?" or "Hello." Yes, all the horrors of war can be forgotten and enemies can be forgotten. We know we must never forget, but I can hardly realize that this Japan is the same one we fought at Okinawa. It must be their trick, for they have almost treated us as liberators.

Lawrence Smith and shipmates at Sasebo, Japan

There is a real show of might in Yokohama. Every standing building uptown is taken over by our Army and Navy. Vacant lots are crowded with Ducks, Trucks, and oil drums, and each building shows it is the headquarters of some port company or division or battalion commander. The roads are always crowded with our trucks, jeeps, and other military vehicles. One day we just traveled back and forth over the city by catching rides in different military vehicles that came along.

By October the 16th, my pal Jack Kellogg and I felt we had seen all the sights, so that evening we went to the ball park to see the USO show. It was a nice day. As the bleachers were filling up, about 15 or 20 Army nurses came in by ones and twos. They were all cheered with the usual whistles and whoops. Most were escorted by majors and colonels, but for some unknown reason, two were with just plain ordinary sailors. Then the rest of the nurses were all escorted by Naval officers. A sailor nearby told me that all those officers and the two sailors were off his ship. They had brought these nurses to Yokohama on their ship, so that accounted for their monopoly.

The stage was two tractor trailer beds side by side. The Army service group was putting up some mikes and speakers. We noticed Danny Kaye down front among the fellows. Some were timidly taking his picture. One of the Army nurses went striding out there. Danny saw her coming, and pushed the crowd back, put his hands in his pockets and stuck his chest way out. The nurse stopped and took a picture of him, then whirled around and went back to her seat.

The Japanese who had gathered around were run out, but a few looked in and watched the show. The persons taking part in the show were Danny Kaye and Leo Durocher, and an Army band. It was a very good show. I would like to see Danny Kaye in his most recent picture, "Wonder Man." As you know Leo Durocher is the manager of the Brooklyn Dodgers and he did okay, too. They had a funny routine where Durocher kicked dirt on an umpire, just as he does at ball games. We were told this was the first USO show in Japan. We surely enjoyed it.

Lawrence

My Letter from Kiirun, Formosa

Kiirun, Formosa, Nov. 30, 1945

Dear Folks,

At Sasebo, Kyushu, Japan, where we arrived on October the 28th, we received some much needed repairs to our ship's bottom. We were supposed to work out of Sasebo on some mine-sweeping operations, but LCS 11 stayed in the harbor the entire time we were there. The mine sweepers break the mines loose from their moorings, and the LCS's come along to blow them up with gunfire. In about ten days LCS 16 destroyed 242 mines. They got 47 in one day. Mines must have been plentiful where they were. Occasionally a ship hits a mine and it is either sunk or damaged badly, but it does not happen often. The mine sweepers and LCS's only work in the day time. After dark they go to a safe area to anchor for the night.

The time I spent at Sasebo was interesting. Toward the end of our stay, dysentery began to spread around, and that made me glad to get away from there. I went into the heart of Sasebo only one time. It was the same old story: a bombed out city with the Japs working and doing things like in the other places we had seen.

LCS 11 at Sasebo, Japan

The area around Sasebo has some low mountains that are covered with small trees. That is where I got my exercise. Many of the men played football in a cleared area not too far from our ship. We were lucky enough to be tied up to a dock where we could get ashore. Every afternoon money was taken up to pay for the beer, and the liberty party went to a certain area set aside for beer drinking, and after that we were more or less on our own. The highest peak in the area was not very far away, and we set out to climb to the top of that peak. Only six of us made the journey. A fellow from St. Louis gave up as the going got tough. This peak is 800 feet high. While up there, we carved our names in the rocks and trees and took some pictures.

The next day I was the SP (Shore Patrol or leader) of our group. In that role I was expected to set an example for the other fellows. Our story of going to the top of that mountain had inspired some of the others of our crew, and this day they wanted to go up there. I didn't really intend to go through all that walking and climbing again, but I gave in and we started in that direction. I took off my SP arm band and pulled my light jacket down over the .45. I didn't think our going up there was the correct thing to do. In case of trouble I was glad to have the "persuader" along. However, the only violence we had heard of happening in the hills was that two soldiers had gotten drunk and one shot the other.

As we reached the top, we found two Buddha shrines. One was a Buddha on a plank table set under some beech trees like the ones over on my Uncle Will's land at the creek. Also there were huge rocks the size of rooms behind the table. This was a nice quiet place. We saw rusted nail points protruding up out of the planks, and the guys thought this was where the worshippers had pricked their heads on these points. They said the greasy spots on the table were caused by their blood. Well, the beer made some of our guys playful, and one said this Buddha would make a nice table piece on our chow table. This thing must have weighed forty or fifty pounds, but we started carrying it down the mountainside across some fields with broom sedge and small pines scattered about. We saw five or six Japs hoeing in a field, and they were looking our way. We draped a guy's jacket around the statue to hide it from them. We were getting tired of carrying this thing and worried about how the Japs might respond, so we ditched it under some low pine sprouts. My friend Kellogg took some pictures of the Japs in the field.

Oh yes, when we first went up to this peak, we felt sure we were the first U. S. people to go up there, but when we got on top, there was a white painted sign that said: "Kilroy was here." This was painted on a rock. We were to see this sign almost everywhere we went.

On another day, some of us who were not playing soccer or football went in another direction and noticed a hill with a flat field on top where broom sedge was growing.

We climbed up there, walked around, and soon found a flat surface with a man-hole cover in it. We looked down under the cover and saw a huge round tank 228 feet in diameter and 48 feet deep. We found some other tanks. Using a ladder, we went down into one. There we found gallon paint cans and picked out a couple of cans to take back and to paint the radio shack floor.

One of the important things that happened at Sasebo was our change of commanding officer. Our captain since the LCS 11 was commissioned had been Lt. Melville E. White. At Sasebo he was made Group Commander. Our executive officer Walter Cameron became our captain. Quite a shuffle was made in the entire crew as far as that goes. About eight men left to go home, and we picked up a couple of replacements. Sasebo happens to be one of the main fleet headquarters. Transportation to the States or to any other point was easy from there. Nagasaki, the city hit by the second atomic bomb, was only about fifty miles away, but none of us got there except one fellow who had some relative in the Army stationed down there.

Another thing that took my interest was the movies we had at Sasebo. Less than 100 feet from our ship was a long narrow concrete building, and this was made into the "Bijou Theater." Our theater was pretty nice. And another thing that came in handy for our crew was that we got a better projector. Our projector was being worked on for over a week, so our Group Commander's projector served both ships. Then to our surprise, we were offered a 35mm projector in exchange for our 16mm. We traded and now have a very nice projector, but the Navy reels are short for the 35, so we have to change reels often. Our old projector would cost $475 new, and the projector we have now would cost from $2500 to $3000 new. While coming down to Kiirun one night we watched a movie. That was something new for an LCS as it is so small that we can't very well operate the ship and have movies going at the same time.

At our "Bijou Theater" I had looked up at the roof when the reels were being changed, and I noticed how meticulously the Japs had used beautiful pine wood for the rafters and cross trusses, Daddy [*a carpenter*] would be impressed. The pine wood was very smooth, and the joints were perfectly joined like cabinet work.

On November the 15th or 16th we learned from "our boy" on the flag ship that we were going to Formosa on the 23rd. He was right, but the date of departure was changed to the 25th. We had a very pleasant trip down. We noticed a change in the weather with every mile. It is very pleasant down here. Before we left Sasebo, we began to get cold early in the mornings, and the weather had a real tinge of fall in it.

We arrived at Kiirun, Formosa, on November the 28th. We expected to see Japs here, but on top of every house, building, and fishing craft is the Chinese flag. The people are of mixed ethnicity, but man-o-man, are they shrewd bargainers! For some old worthless Japanese coin, they want a *pack* of cigarettes. Inflation is so great that it takes hundreds and hundreds of Chinese "dollars" to equal an American dollar. To add to the confusion, the Chinese communists have issued money, the Japs have issued money, and the Chinese Nationalists have issued money, until you really don't know which is good and which isn't. Little kids were bringing out bills with 1000 Yuan written on them; we had not come in contact with them before. And firecrackers—you would think the war was still going on, as they are continually popping. Every kid has a couple hundred in varying sizes.

Begging for food here is also a specialized art. Around meal time hundreds of Chinese line up with their little buckets and baskets. It makes you almost dread to take your tray topside, to know you will be mobbed. Each nest of ships has a man who walks along the dock with a carbine, standing guard. These fellows on guard duty never say anything to us when we give stuff to the kids. Naturally that draws them to the ship. If I were standing guard, I would try to keep the sailors from drawing that crowd instead of just trying to keep the crowd back.

What made me angry at one of the guards was his use of the hose to run the mob back. He didn't wet so many, but it was like herding animals or something. I guess people in the United States will never realize what a different world they live in compared to many other countries. In these mobs were not only kids, but all ages up to old men and women. I noticed a woman with a shifty look. She laughed nervously and kept a constant lookout to see if any food was being handed out anywhere. When a wastebasket was emptied in a barrel up the dock, all the crowd around us scattered like chickens running to the place where a farmer had just thrown a bunch of grain. Even though they behave as though they are starving, they have plenty of bananas to trade.

Some of our cooks made a trade for fresh green beans, eggs and some other items to give us fresh food, but when some officers found out about it, they told us not to do that. They said it was not safe for us to eat these foods. The people here use human manure, and it was feared that some disease (like the dysentery at Sasebo) would be spread to us.

The landscape is about the same as that of Japan so far as I have seen it. I have not been on a liberty yet. We had a movie on the dock. We set up our screen and projector out there. The show was "The Mask of Dimitreus," or however that is spelled. Judging by the attendance of the natives on Formosa, I would say they surely liked the picture.

As I have been writing this, we have been shooting at what we at first thought was a mine, but it turned out to be a net buoy. It sank. We have been sweeping this area since last night. This area has been swept once already, so we don't expect to find much. This job will only last two days. Then we will go back into Kiirun.

We have heard that if the monsoon rains hold off, the Seventh Fleet will have its areas swept by Christmas. We are to go to Shanghai for Christmas. They mentioned this like going to Shanghai would be a real treat, so we are rather looking forward to it. We are temporarily attached to the Seventh Fleet. We have been in the Fifth, the Third, and the Seventh Fleet now. These are the main fleets of the Pacific. It will be interesting to see how we continue to operate under the fast changing conditions of men going home and our needing replacements. But I know we will get by somehow—at least we always have. Some say we will be heading for the States after this operation, but I believe it is only wishful thinking. Also there are tales that the only reason we are out here now is that the ports back at the States are too crowded to take care of us if we were to return now. No one knows what the future holds, but we don't worry and do lots of joking about fighting a new war up the Yangtze River.

With a full war-time complement, we had about sixty-six enlisted men and six to eight officers. About the time we reached Aomori, the complement was lowered to fifty men and six officers. At Sasebo we learned that the actual complement of an LCS is thirty-six men and four officers. All this means is that the guns aren't cleaned as often as they used to be. No guns are manned when we are underway. Only about three lookouts are on duty. We have two signalmen and one quartermaster. They do each other's jobs. We got rid of two quartermasters and one signalman. This means more work for all of us left aboard. But we aren't expected to do as much or do it quite as efficiently as when we were fully manned in wartime.

Well, if you are still awake by the time you have read to here, you will notice I am about to say Goodbye until next time.

Love,
Your son, Lawrence

MY LETTER FROM SHANGHAI, 1945

After mine sweeping in the Pescadores, LCS 11 sailed to Shanghai, arriving at the mouth of the Yangtze in late December. Mr. Walt Cameron was now skipper of the ship having been promoted from executive officer to that position a couple months earlier, after Mel White had been made commander of LCS Group 8. Mr. Cameron recalls an incident aboard the ship shortly after we tied up in Shanghai: "I wonder how many of our guys remember what was going on in the steering engine room within minutes after we docked in Shanghai just before Christmas 1945! I had to break it up, but my God, the ingenuity and enterprise!"

Sid Darion responded: "As to Walt's reference to the extracurricular activities in the steering engine room when we docked in Shanghai, I remember it well."

The black gang even managed to get mattresses and some kind of incense going; I think that helped give the action away. I vividly remember Fritz Henry's frantic dash to the bridge with the anguished cry, "Captain, we've got a floating whore house!" I know Captain Cameron had to break it up, but don't feel too bad, Walt. The charter members of the "House of the Fantail Fling" were exhausted by the time you had to act.

Shanghai, Dec 31, 1945

Dear folks,

Here it is the end of the year 1945 —the year that was the Victory Year. The year's end finds me in Shanghai, China. This is the PARIS of the Far East. On leaving Kiirun, Formosa, on December the 18th we had the Group Commander [Melvin White] aboard LCS 11. This only gave us more work, but "Steamer" (our old skipper and now the LCS Group 8 Commander) brought along a signalman and a radioman to help us out.

I had the 4 to 8 watch on the morning of December 21. I noticed the dark or rather reddish color of the water [*off the coast of China*]. Seeing this kind of landscape was certainly a new experience for me. The sun was shining, and it looked like a beautiful morning except for some fog up ahead. It seemed we would never get to the entrance of the Yangtze River but around noon we anchored near it. When we started out again, it seemed like a different world, for the sun wasn't shining; and it was cold. As we continued up the river, it got colder. I nearly froze to death trying to get just a glimpse of China. A ferry dipped its flag to us as we met. We tied up to an oiler for the night and took on water and fuel.

In the morning we moved on toward town on the Wangapoo River, a tributary of the Yangtze. This river isn't over half a mile wide anywhere, and it surely seemed strange to see all the buildings on both sides. We passed some cruisers and AGC's (Amphibious Group Command ships) and went by the main buildings going on up the river. Naturally our little amphibious craft would go miles from the Liberty Landing. We moved along the wrong (or left) side of the river. We are two miles south of the Liberty Landing, yet we are above the city. Sheds, buildings, and warehouses come right out to the edge of the water. The roofs show signs such as: "Pootung Dry Docks Co., Wahung and Chia Tu Ting" and such other signs in English that sound so Chinese.

When we neared the area of downtown, we saw hundreds of junks on both sides of the river, and as we were barely moving, many of these craft came up on each side of our ship wanting to sell us something. I thought our officers would do something to keep these junks away, but they more or less put up with them after some half-hearted shouts to keep them away from the ship. Some of these Chinese climbed up on the ship. They scrambled aboard to sell anything from suitcases and trunks to scarves and rings and watches, and we had to shoo them back off.

But I really learned something. I heard some of the knowledgeable guys speak of "sloe" gin—well, it surely wasn't "slow" because a bunch of our guys were intoxicated in short order. Bernard Michaelson, a radioman, came in the radio shack and lay on the floor and beat it with his fists, saying over and over something about "not wanting to hurt anybody." He would name some of our guys, especially one of our radiomen, but it didn't make any sense to me.

The river runs fairly swiftly and is always very brown. It is usually littered with a variety of sampans, fishing boats, tugs, and junks. I read in an English newspaper that there used to be many bodies in the river in some areas. For a while the government offered a $25 reward to those bringing in the bodies, but at that price it appeared people were throwing other people into the river to collect the $25, so they had to quit that award system.

There are several British ships and one French heavy cruiser here. Since these ships are parked so near downtown, I guess their electricians have to keep up appearances. I noticed some pretty nifty Christmas lights on their ships. I had never seen anything like it aboard a ship before. I guess the mine sweepers must have special lights, for they have red and green lights in sets from the top of their masts to the deck, and these lights flash on and off at regular intervals. Some have winking stars. There are some really nice ones.

I went on my first liberty in Shanghai on December the 22nd. Shanghai really is a change for fellows who have, for a year, not been to a city where they could spend money. The cities we visited in Japan were all blown apart and there was nothing in the stores that were still standing.

Cigarettes bring various prices. The producers of Camel cigarettes could feel very conceited if they saw the preference here for Camels over the other brands. I remember for some particular article the natives had to sell they wanted six cartons of Chesterfields or four cartons of Camels for the object. This is the usual ratio. Chesterfields bring about 3 dollars per carton and Camels bring about 5 dollars. But there is no open sale of them as I have noted. It is black-market to deal in them.

We were met at the jetty by men, women, and children selling scarves, rings, and watches. We walked down streets like those of Boston and by stores that seem to have a more plentiful supply of goods than those in the U. S. We were amazed at the silk goods and such things as Hohner harmonicas and things that the States don't have. There are modern bakeries, shoe stores, and fur stores. Window displays show many modern items for sale. I was surprised to see new typewriters on display. There are hat stores and all of the specialty stores. There are modern night clubs, theaters, and hotels.

There are quite a few 1942 Buicks, Chevrolets, Studebakers, Plymouths, and Chryslers around Shanghai and they really look new. It makes us wonder where they came from. On January the 1st traffic will change over from the left-hand side of the street to the right-hand side. I wonder how that will work out.

Shanghai is certainly a large city, and you can readily believe all reports of a large Chinese population, for the streets are crowded most of the time. The thousands of rickshaws are a new spectacle for me. Seeing these two-wheeled carts being pulled by runners is something that makes me certain that I am in the Orient. They weave in and out of traffic and compete with the smaller number of automotive vehicles.

Sex is for sale in a different way here. You don't see the girls on the streets. Young boys, appearing to be about 10-15 years old, approach and cry out to passing servicemen: "You want school girl? Young school girl? My sister! School girl." Evidently "school" is a keyword connoting youth, vitality, and knowledge. Some women in their kimono-type dress approach servicemen early in the day, but the young boys are very active as hucksters in the early evening.

Chinese money is a topic for a book in itself. Any money that has "Reserve" on it is no good. Money that says "Gold Certificate" on it is worth twenty times what the bill says on its face. Bills of the same worth are of many different sizes and colors. Some say Bank of China, Bank of Communications, and others say Farmers Bank of China. Yuan is the Chinese equivalent of our dollar and is the only Chinese money that is used as far as I know. Chinese money is known as CN or CNC (Chinese National Currency).

If you have read the December 24th issue of Time magazine, you noted that the Chinese have jacked up their prices, especially because of the sailors that have swarmed ashore in Shanghai. American money is respected like gold. But it's best to have your money changed for you by someone you trust. You are easily cheated because the Chinese like to give you change in their money.

Since inflation is high, it takes 100 Yuan to amount to any money at all. A five Yuan bill is worth less than one-half American cent. The rate of exchange is different every day. The first day I went on liberty, an American dollar was worth 1260 Yuan. Yesterday it was worth 1410. If their money is not in denominations of 1000, it really takes a stack of it to be worth anything at all. For example, the newspaper Stars and Stripes costs 50 Yuan.

The Red Cross operates from the foreign YMCA and does a good job. Also, the Navy Enlisted Men's Club is very well run and can accommodate a large number of men. I had my first fresh tomatoes in a year and a half at this club. These places are very nice for getting away from the street vendors who swarm around you like flies. I guess the American sailor has gained the reputation of being vulnerable to the sales tactics of the Chinese. I was walking behind an Army guy up Nanking Street. Both of us were by ourselves and walking rather fast. The Army guy was approached only about three times with scarves, rings, and such; whereas practically everybody tried to sell me something.

Although there were supposed to be no settlements of foreigners here like before the war, there are sections still considered the French Settlement, Russian, American, and such. The Russians rank second in population and in control of Shanghai. The favorite drink is Vodka. There are quite a few men from India with their tall, husky bodies, black beards, and turbans.

There isn't as much of the weird-type music and smoking long pipes as I have seen in movies about China. Some of it is really pretty. The English language is fairly well known and such songs as "Candy" and "Sentimental Journey" are sung by some of the Chinese girls at the theaters and clubs. They have several very nice theaters. Such pictures as "Aloma of the South Seas," "Beau Gests," and "Greenwich Village" are playing at the theaters— all first class pictures! I guess the Chinese are making up for what they missed during the war.

I went on liberty December the 22nd, 24th, 25th, 26th, 28th, and 30th. On one of these trips I had some pictures made at a studio and will send you a couple. One night I went with several of my shipmates to a night club where a band was playing. We had some vodka and coke and a very nice meal. One of our radiomen, having had too much to drink, went up on the bandstand and took over the drummer's place. He drew lots of applause at first for his ability, but he ruined his performance by throwing up on the musicians near him.

I have gone everywhere by walking except one short rickshaw ride. I walked way, way out Bubbling Well Road. It was a chilly day with the temperature around freezing. Along the way I saw five different men lying on the sidewalk trembling and shaking, and everyone just walked around or over them, just as if they might have been a crack in the sidewalk. I thought how different this was from America where someone would have called an ambulance or tried to assist them.

Way out this road I went into the Enlisted Men's Club for a while. An old salt Chief and three other servicemen were playing cards and drinking beer. As they emptied their cans of beer, they added the cans to a pyramid of empty cans. Evidently they had been playing for a very long time, because the pyramid was about four feet high and still growing.

Another strange thing: While we have been here, a Chinese boy has been spending most days aboard the LCS 11. He is Leo Estrada and has a Shanghai address. I think he is part Spanish or Italian. Some of the guys are very friendly to him and have "adopted" him, and he says he wants to come to the United States with us.

Well, folks, I have told about all there is to tell. For further information, you would have to hear the sounds and smell the smells for yourself.

Love, your son,
Lawrence

About our stay in Shanghai, G. O. Davis says, "The liberties we had together were some of the best days of my life. I remember Paul Weir and a couple of us rented rickshaws in Shanghai, and we bought firecrackers which we threw under the heels of the gooks pulling us as we had a race down main street. Paul and I grabbed at each other and the wheels broke. The men who pulled us got rather mad at us for the damage we did."

Paul Weir replied, "I remember that rickshaw ride and the wreck. Those Chinese were jumping around and hollering as we walked away, 'Who is going to pay?' That was on the way from the Royal Bar. I don't know who was in the race down the main drag. We put the coolie in the rickshaw, and we raced down the street. It was fun!"

SHIPMATE'S LETTER
ABOUT SHANGHAI

In the letter below Sid Darion, our radio technician, recalls going ashore when LCS 11 was moored at Shanghai in late December 1945 and early January 1946.

Dear Smygly,

Your letter home from Shanghai brought back a lot of memories. I have a batch of that old Chinese currency squirreled away somewhere. You remember how the rate of exchange would vary from day to day and even hour to hour. Well, thereby hangs a tale.

Scotty Rogers and I helped a Navy man in need out of a fight. The man was very appreciative. Turns out he was a Chief Warrant Officer and lived in a nearby hotel. This was somewhere on Bubbling Well Road, no more than a half mile from the docks. The CWO invited us to his room while he cleaned up and then said we'd go for drinks in the hotel cocktail lounge.

When we got to his room, he went into the bathroom to wash while Scotty and I attacked a Scotch bottle. Then Scotty noticed that one of the drawers in a chest of drawers was partly open. It was hard not to see what was in it. It was jammed full of U. S. currency—and it was a big drawer. We pretended like we had not noticed anything, but we realized later that our host had guessed that we had, even though he nudged the drawer closed.

We had our drinks at the lounge, and he introduced us to a lot of people as friends who had saved his ass. That made us their friends. He also introduced us to "The Fat Man" who ran an elaborate whore house on the upper floors of the hotel. Scotty and I were "honored guests "up there several times. We even had the options of asking for girls "Short time, long time, or all night."

I can't remember whether we shared any of this with the guys on the ship because we were sworn to secrecy. Turns out the CWO was a Navy paymaster with access to a plane. He was responsible for a Navy payroll in Shanghai and another in a city about 40 miles away. Because of bandits and such, traveling by road was out. The only way to transport currency safely was by plane, and he had one of the few available.

There was a consistent exchange difference between Shanghai and the other city he serviced. So this guy was playing the entire Navy payrolls he handled on the money market and keeping the profits. The police chief of Shanghai was in on the act. He had brought in the mayor and some other money people including the owner of a department store outlet in San Francisco. Our CWO's wife, in San Francisco, became an officer in the company. CWO's profits were handed over in San Francisco—no transfer of funds from China that could be traced to him. It was a setup so lucrative, he was seriously considering re-enlisting. Said he couldn't afford to give up the golden goose. I realized later that this combine was undoubtedly contributing to the collapse of Chinese currency, but Scotty and I were not that sophisticated at the time.

Rogers and I were wined and dined and saw no reason for blowing the whistle on our friend. One of the exciting results of this strange relationship was our being invited to a New Years Eve Party the likes of which I haven't seen since. Scotty and I were picked up at dockside by one of the police chief's limos. I remember not being scheduled for liberty that night and pleading my case not to disappoint the police chief and mayor. The OD (officer of the deck)—I think it was Fritz Henry, didn't believe me of course. But he did say, "Darion, if the limo comes for you right here where I can see it, you can go." Well, come it did, and off Scotty and I went.

The banquet was sensational and I couldn't identify anything on the plates. There must have been thirty people there, and I think each person had his own waiter. Also it was my first introduction to chop sticks. I would have starved if a kind and very attractive woman sitting next to me hadn't fed me.

This is also where we were introduced to the pleasures of "kan-pay." That's a phonetic spelling. Anyway, it was done with hot rice wine. Somebody looked at me and toasted, "Kan-pay, Sid." I then had to chugalug my drink and kanpay someone else. If I was slow, and I was, I would be kanpayed again and again. And I was. Scotty and I got quite bombed.

Another exotic experience that night was the duck's head. As an honored guest I got to crack it between my teeth and suck out the brains. It was very bad form to refuse. Fortunately, I was in no pain at the time so I did it to much applause.

Another recollection of Shanghai is one that Hammond might remember. Somewhere a group of us got hold of a huge cigar— a four-foot stodgy. We marched up Bubbling Well Road with me smoking it at the end and several of the guys smoking it from the sides with cigarette holders they jammed into it. Behind us came Hammond beating a drum. I can't remember where he got the drum. And as we marched puffing and drumming, kids started to follow us. I think we wound up leading a parade of half the kids in the area before we peeled off for some liquid refreshment. Ring a bell, Chuck?

Smygly, what memories you bring back! You know, what strikes me odd now is that I have told that first story many times. I have written about it. I even worked parts of it into a TV script. The only people I haven't shared it with are the guys on this ship who were there when it all happened. I'm sure Scotty and I talked about the dinner afterwards, but we never did tell anyone about the CWO's operation till much, much later. Well, I never would have had a chance to share it with you guys if you hadn't started this great project of yours.

Note from quartermaster Willis "Scotty" Rogers to Darion: *At that famous New Years Eve party: When it came time for the "duck's head" there was a debate over who was "guest of honor," you or me. I flipped a coin and announced that you had won the toss, but didn't show the coin. Now I can admit I won the toss, but didn't have the nerve for the duck's head. I've wanted to tell you this for a long time. I must have been a little less drunk than you. Boy, that hot rice wine was good.*

Sasebo to Manila, 1946

On January 3, 1946, we departed Shanghai aboard LCS 11 and arrived at the outer harbor of Sasebo, Japan, on January the 5th. By January the 8th we were in a floating dry dock. On the 11th we left the dry dock and tied up at Charlie dock. Our ship was being prepared for her trip back across the Pacific to the States. On the 12th we were docked at No. 2 Graving dry dock.

At Sasebo, Doc Dobbs did a big favor for a member of our crew. While we were in dry dock, one of the guys accidentally shot himself in the leg with his pistol. He went to Doc Dobbs for treatment and begged Doc not to report the accidental shooting. Dobbs covered for him, telling our officers that the guy had the flu or something while he was secretly nursing the crewman back to health. The fact that the guy lived shows how skilled our corpsman was.

LCS 11 in dry dock at Sasebo, Japan, 1946

On January 14, 1946, at Sasebo, I learned I was leaving LCS 11. And on the 15th I was transferred to PGM 13. I don't know what PGM stood for. As I remember, the mission of these boats was to patrol coastlines, inland bays and rivers, and to rescue downed pilots close to shore.

Several other crewmen from LCS 11 were transferred at the same time. I can't remember who else was transferred off the Eleven and went aboard PGM 13 with me, but Creekmur and Borsch certainly did because later they were with me in the flight from Palawan to Manila. Kellogg said he was also transferred to a PGM. My entry for February 11, says PGM 12, 13, and 21 left Sasebo at the same time for the Philippines. But there were others leaving at different times including PGM 22, PGM 28, and LSM 495. I remember seeing Willis Rogers in a photo given to me by Kellogg. It was taken aboard a PGM lovingly named "Lacanuki" and that was painted on the wheel house. So Rogers must have been on the PGM with Kellogg.

We lived aboard PGM 13 in Sasebo Harbor for almost a month before sailing for the Philippines. During that time, on January 25th, we watched LCS 11 pull out for the States. Some new crew members had been assigned to her, but several of the old hands were still aboard. Before the Lucky Eleven pulled out, a ceremony honoring her service was held. The program brought back a flood of memories of my days spent on her.

Then on February 11, 1946, on board PGM 13, in the company of PGM's 12 and 21, some of my LCS 11 shipmates and I left Sasebo for the Philippines. I was pleased to be going there again. Following the Battle of Okinawa, we had spent some time at Leyte waiting for the invasion of Japan to begin. I note with interest the entry in my log for February 13, 1946, which says, "We passed just to the west of Okinawa and saw Ibehya Shima and Kerma Retto." As we passed the islands, I remembered some of the things we had experienced there during the Okinawa campaign. LCS 11 had escorted a PBM to its base at Kerma Retto. We also went to Kerma Retto for repairs after we had run aground on June 4, 1945.

We arrived at Puerto Princessa, Palawan, in the Southwest Philippine Islands on February 15th. A kind of melancholy came over me as I walked around under thick palms on a place where a base had been located during the war. The palms were like a roof overhead, and no grass grew underneath. The sand was sugar-white, and tables had been built between two trees near each hut. I guess these tables were where the men ate their meals. But not a soul was thereabouts now, and the place had been left very clean and neat. At the air base nearby I enjoyed watching P-51 mustangs land and take off. They reminded me of angry wasps back on the farm. But there were only a few of these planes, and some C-47's painted that dull khaki green-brown.

Several other crewmen and I from LCS 11 stayed aboard PGM 13 in the harbor of Puerto Princessa through the first week of March. On the 6th we got word that we were eligible to leave. We packed our gear and prepared for a flight to Manila. The officers had made preparations for us to leave the next day. I got paid $150.

But the next morning—the 7th— we began to run into problems. First, the 0800 boat that was supposed to take us ashore didn't run. Next, when we finally got ashore, the truck that was to take us to the airstrip wouldn't start, and when we did get to the field, the plane cancelled its 0915 flight. We were then scheduled to board the 1130 plane for Samar. But that plane was late; so we ate chow. The plane never showed up, and nobody seemed to know why. We returned to PGM 13 for the night, marveling at our bad luck.

Arriving back aboard PGM 13 seemed strange to me because we thought we had said our last goodbye to that ship. Creekmur had borrowed some money from one of the guys, and when we came back on board, the lender clapped his hands and said, "Well, Jim, I'm glad to see you didn't wait long to look me up and pay your debt!"

The next day, March 8th, we tried it again. We left the ship at 0800, went to the Red Cross and at 1030 reported to the MATS (Military Air Transport Service) office. It was pouring down rain. A MATS plane flew overhead, but it went on to Manila without landing because—as we were told— the visibility was too low. But then we saw an Army C-47 approach the field and land. After having our noon chow, we came back to the air strip. By then, the skies were starting to clear, and we were getting desperate. When we learned that the Army C-47 was going to Manila, Creekmur decided to talk to the plane's crew about our hitching a ride with them. And, after much talking, we were allowed to board "Carmelia," the Army C-47.

We took off about 1325. The plane on which we hitched a ride had two pieces of wood down each side in the fuselage with strips of canvas stretched between. These were our seats. We flew low— I would guess around 5,000 feet. We could look out and see the white foamy water breaking against the northern side of the many small islands surrounded by the blue water. We hit one rough spot of weather; otherwise it was a very pleasant trip. Visibility was good, so we landed at Neilson Field, Manila, about 1530. The only passengers on the trip were Creekmur, Bosch, an Army lieutenant and myself.

We were surprised that the Naval Air Transport Service used such a flimsy excuse as poor visibility when they didn't land for us, because the Army planes on the base were flying in and out. But Creekmur was so elated about his ability to persuade the Army boys to let us hitch a ride to Manila that he didn't want to check in with the Navy officials. He just wanted to hitch-hike by plane all the way to the States. But I was afraid we might end up in Alaska or South America.

We traveled then to COMPHILSEAFRON base with our sea bags, rifles (these were Japanese rifles we were taking home as souvenirs), and orders. I found a bunk, and we began to explore the station and its surroundings, looking for entertainment. We visited a beer garden and then went to a movie. It was quite a day. Our plane trip had taken two hours. If we had sailed on PGM 13, it would have taken 30 hours. This night of March the 8th marked the first time we had slept on land since December 23, 1944. As I went to bed that night I heard dishes or trays rattling at the mess hall nearby, and in the wee hours of the morning I heard jeeps revving their engines. I had to admit that these sounds weren't as soothing as the steady hum of the air blowers which had lulled me to sleep in compartments aboard ship.

THE FINAL VOYAGE
OF LCS 11

During the occupation of Japan, we had visited Aomori, Yokohama, Yokosuka, Tokyo, and Sasebo. Then we exploded mines behind mine sweepers off the Pescadores Islands and visited Shanghai for Christmas in 1945. The crew of the Lucky Eleven went our separate ways from Sasebo, Japan, in early 1946. A few stayed aboard the ship a while longer, and some new members were assigned to help bring her back to the States. I went to the Philippines on PGM 13 and took a flight with Creekmur and Borsch to Neilson Field at Manila. From there I sailed in LCI 464 to Cavite and on to Subic Naval Base. Then aboard *Santa Monica*, I went by Samar and Guam to San Francisco. I left San Francisco on my birthday, April 8th, and arrived at Charleston, South Carolina, on April 13th. I had a physical exam on Sunday and was discharged and went home on Monday, April the 15th.

Shipmate George Blasius stayed with LCS (3) 11 to her final port, and below he summarizes the ship's activities in 1946:

Left Shanghai, China, at 0940 on the 3rd of January;
Arrived at Sasebo, Kyushu, Japan, at 2000 on the 5th of
*   January;*
(Throughout the entire mine-sweeping operation in this
*   period, we sank 3 mines, and 4 buoys)*
Detached from Mine Pack at 830 on 21st of January;
Left Sasebo, Japan, at 1400 on the 25th of January;
Arrived at 1930 on 31st of January at Saipan, Mariana
*   Islands;*
Left Saipan at 1745 on 9th of February;
Arrived at 0815 at Eniwetok, Atoll, Marshall Islands, on
*   16th of February;*
Left at 0715 Eniwetok on 17th of February;
Arrived at Pearl Harbor, Hawaiian Islands, on 28th of
*   February;*
Left Pearl on 21st of March;
Arrived San Francisco, California, on March 30th.

At San Francisco George Blasius was transferred from the ship on the 16th of April to Treasure Island. Next he traveled to the Great Lakes Base, Illinois, where he arrived April the 23rd. He was discharged from the Navy on April 28, 1946.

Some crew members joined the ship and served just long enough to help bring her back to the States. Gerald "Jerry" Hoye writes in a letter: "my assignment on the USS LCS 11 was very brief. In February and March of 1946 I had enough points to be discharged, and I was transferred to the LCS 11 for a voyage home from Sasebo, Japan. I remember it was a long, long, long trip with many engine breakdowns on the way. For a period of several days, the sea was absolutely calm, flat as a mirror. We arrived at San Francisco on April 1, 1946. I've never forgotten seeing the towers of the Golden Gate Bridge appearing above the cloud and fog bank. I had a hard time believing I had actually survived the war."

Paul Weir, Scotty Rogers, Kellogg, and I among others, were transferred to different ships at Sasebo, Japan. Scotty, a quartermaster from the Lucky Eleven, went aboard PGM

22 which was bound for Hawaii. Scotty says, "I remember I conned the captain into not making me stand watch by agreeing to take morning and evening position sights. Paul Weir would come down and wake me an hour before sun-up, and when I'd dressed and put on my shoes, he would tell me it was raining and there were no stars visible." Scotty adds,

I remember I spent the whole trip playing cribbage in the engine room with the chief motor mac. I seem to remember Paul Weir and Reginald Hill swinging baseball bats trying to kill rats in the officer's cabin; and I remember Knock-about and me squirting bug spray. Boy, that ship was dirty!

Paul recounts that he left Sasebo on a PGM but that he didn't know which one it was. Scotty Rogers replied that the PGM was number 22. That puts Kellogg, Rogers, and Weir on the same ship destined for Hawaii. Weir says, "We left Sasebo, Japan, on that PGM at flank speed" and remembers his trip to Hawaii and the States this way:

We traveled alone for a while. But that didn't last too long as we got orders to escort a crippled APD to Pearl. The skipper of the APD outranked our skipper, and we toured the Pacific Ocean while he took pictures for a book he was going to write. I recall Gunter was a cook on there. The range broke; it was over-worked, and I don't remember how many days we ate corn beef hash. We finally arrived at Pearl. A few days out of port our skipper decided that the PGM should be sharp when it got to Pearl. The Bosun broke out the paint and everything that went with it and ordered all hands to turn to. All that happened was that the ocean depth rose from all that paint, hammers, and so forth, that went overboard. Seeing no progress, the skipper asked Boats [the Bosun] what was wrong, and Boats told him all hands were petty officers going home for discharge and couldn't care less about the ship. Upon arrival at Pearl, the skipper went ashore and got replacements for all hands. We didn't spend a night in the outgoing unit. We flew out that night on a C-54 for San Francisco. Because of weight limits, I left all my souvenirs there and took just a suitcase.

LCS 11 went to San Francisco to be decommissioned, arriving at the end of March. The deck log for Saturday, March 30, 1946, reports in the midnight-to-0400 watch, signed by B. B. Vedder, Jr., that the ship was underway in formation 500 yards to port of APC 27, the guide ship for the formation. LCS (L) 17 was 500 yards astern of LCS 11. How about that! LCS 17 was the ship I lived aboard for several days at Aomori without its skipper and my own skipper knowing about it. The 0800 to 1200 watch says: "Underway on various courses and speeds entering San Francisco Harbor." And finally at 1245 LCS 11 "Moored starboard to LCS (L) 16" in Anchorage 6-3.

On Tuesday April the 2nd twenty men were transferred off LCS 11 to the US Naval Receiving Station at Treasure Island for discharge. Gerald Hoye was in that group that included the LCS 11 regulars Sidney Darion, Elmer Jensen, Everitt L. Terwilliger and George Robert Waldron. The next day, ten more were transferred off. Among them were Dewey Fussell and James E. Hayes.

LCS 11 reached San Franciso under the command of Walter Cameron. He was the second skipper of the ship, having been moved up from executive officer when White took command of Group 8 in the fall of 1945 at Sasebo. It's fair to say that Cameron did not put as much of a barrier between himself and the crew as White had done as skipper. Darion remembers "leaning over the bow rail one evening while Skipper Cameron told me about his experiences in Normandy. I was amazed that he could be moved from one active war theater to another so quickly. I also remember having very good feelings about him as our C. O. There were no airs or bullshit about him. He was a friendly, competent commander who got our respect without a sledge hammer. I know I felt comfortable with him on the bridge."

Other officers still aboard the Eleven when she got to San Francisco were Vedder, Henry, and Kehrwald. Some enterprising photographer took a picture of LCS ll as she came into San Francisco Bay. About that photograph Mr.Vedder says, "You'll note at least one hose hanging over the side discharging water, an example of the many mechanical failures the Eleven suffered on the long voyage home."

By April 15, 1946, most of us were civilians again. We sent each other Christmas cards for a while and then we drifted away. Fortunately, while we were at Shanghai, Sid Darion and Willis Rogers thought of writing and distributing a "yearbook" of our crew. Sid, one of the really good writers in our crew, wrote the following about the log:

The war over and time on our hands in Shanghai, Scotty and I got the idea for writing a ship's log something like the graduation books we got in high school. We got enthusiastic support from the communications gang and out came that booklet with everybody's name and address and a paragraph about each of the crew members. Scotty and I spent long and happy days and nights putting that together. I'm amazed at the quality when I look at it today.

As an example of the paragraphs written about crew members, here is what the Log says about Ernest G. Kupfer, EM 1/c our electrician story-teller from Cleveland, Ohio: "The Old Man was always ready with a sea story, and he'd split a pint with anybody. Always popular, Kup was respected as an electrician who really knew his job. He was always ready for a spot of tea in the evening, and anyone who thought Kup was really old, changed his mind if he happened to be in the passageway when the Old Man made one of his famous dashes for the generator room."

The mast-head page shows that Sid and Scotty wrote most of the text for the 42-page Log; Bob Faller and Jim "Spanky" Creekmur did the art work; Chuck Hammond, Junior Dennis, Lawrence Smith, and Curtis Pace typed and produced it. We used stencils and a mimeograph machine. The Lucky Eleven Log (or as it has sometimes been called *The Shanghai Log*) was to be a great help to me when I began to search for members of the crew on June 26, 1987.

The value of our experiences together on the ship through the war is remarkable. It may partly be explained by the intensity of sharing life-threatening dangers and of living in close proximity to each other. We grew to depend on one another in times of danger and became good friends in times of recreation. In the process, our days together took on a large importance in our lives. Our reunions forty-odd years later confirm that. As Blair Vedder put it, "The crew of the Eleven is one of the finest, friendliest groups of people I've ever had the luck to be associated with. The experience on that rust bucket created an amazing family."

Ship's Roster

OFFICERS

Walter C. Cameron, Jr.
Leonard Covert
Warren C. Eades
Frederick John Henry, Jr.
Clement V. Kehrwald
James C. MacLennan
William L. McCrea
Thomas A. Smith
Beverly Blair Vedder, Jr.
Melvin Ernest White

ENLISTED

Fred N. Allen
John W. Balash
John Belcastro
George W. Blasius
Thomas M. Borst
Rudolph Bosca
Charles H. Breese
Donald Carlile
Adam E. Carter
Francis L. Cavanaugh

Daniel L. Chapman
Richard Choike
James W. Creekmur
Sidney Darion
Woodrow W. Davie
Glenn O. Davis
Ira J. Davis
Emmet L. Dennis
Joseph A. Dennis, Jr.
Douglas R. Deschaine
James C Devol
Charles Dubois
Floyd Eaton
William K. Eversole, Jr.
Robert A. Faller
William F. Fandel
Martin J. Francis
Dewey Fussell
Louis H. Gilliam
Leonard E. Guempelein
Taylor G. Guinn
Hoyle Gunter
Charles G. Hammond
William J. Hanrahan
James Ernest Hayes
Reginald W. Hill
George S. Hopkins
Elmer L. Jensen
Alex Kaskus
Jack Kellogg
Francis Krishko
Ernest G. Kupfer
John Travis Lynn, Jr.
Russell W. Mace
Alexander Marinello
Bernard L. Michaelson
Daryle Keith Mong
Harry L. Murray

Curtis R. Pace
Ernest J. Patenaude, Jr.
Adrian E. Perkins
Raymond V. Reed
George F. Rienas
Willis Rogers
Robert W. Russell
Ernest A. Sako
Edward L. Smith
Kenneth G. Smith
Lawrence B. Smith
Albert Snobelen
Tom King Taylor
Everett K. Terwilliger
Joseph A. Ventura
Merle R. Vertheen
George Robert Waldron
John P. Walsh
Paul H. Weir
Roy L. Wilson
Marvin P. Wissmann

A few others spent just weeks or days aboard the ship.